D1480331

How Science CHANGED THE WORLD

How Antibiotics Changed the World

Toney Allman

ReferencePoint Press®

San Diego, CA

About the Author

Toney Allman holds degrees from The Ohio State University and the University of Hawaii. She currently lives in Virginia, where she enjoys a rural lifestyle as well as researching and writing about a variety of topics for students.

© 2019 ReferencePoint Press, Inc.
Printed in the United States

For more information, contact:
ReferencePoint Press, Inc.
PO Box 27779
San Diego, CA 92198
www.ReferencePointPress.com

ALL RIGHTS RESERVED.
No part of this work covered by the copyright hereon may be reproduced or used in any form or by any means—graphic, electronic, or mechanical, including photocopying, recording, taping, web distribution, or information storage retrieval systems—without the written permission of the publisher.

LIBRARY OF CONGRESS CATALOGING-IN-PUBLICATION DATA

Names: Allman, Toney, author.
Title: How Antibiotics Changed the World/by Toney Allman.
Description: San Diego, CA: ReferencePoint Press, Inc., 2019. | Series: How Science Changed the World series | Audience: Grades 9 to 12. | Includes bibliographical references and index.
Identifiers: LCCN 2018023002 (print) | LCCN 2018023198 (ebook) | ISBN 9781682824061 (eBook) | ISBN 9781682824054 (hardback)
Subjects: LCSH: Antibiotics—Side effects—Juvenile literature.
Classification: LCC RM267 (ebook) | LCC RM267 .A47 2019 (print) | DDC 615.3/29—dc23
LC record available at https://lccn.loc.gov/2018023002

CONTENTS

IMPORTANT EVENTS IN THE HISTORY OF ANTIBIOTICS

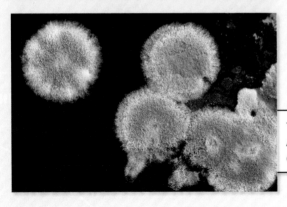

1942
Howard Florey, Ernst Chain, and Norman Heatley invent a process for purifying and manufacturing penicillin. Penicillin is first sold as an antibiotic drug.

1928
Alexander Fleming discovers penicillin.

1944
Selman Waksman discovers the antibiotic streptomycin, which can treat tuberculosis.

1683
Antonie Van Leeuwenhoek becomes the first person to see and describe bacteria.

1870
Louis Pasteur and Robert Koch prove the germ theory of disease.

| 1680 | / | 1860 | 1890 | 1920 | 1950 |

1909
Paul Ehrlich discovers a chemical compound that kills syphilis bacteria.

1932
Gerhard Domagk discovers a class of dyes that come to be known as sulfonamides and slow the growth of bacterial infections.

1950
Widespread use of antibiotics as growth promoters for food animals becomes common.

1955
Tetracycline, the first broad spectrum antibiotic made by chemically altering a natural antibiotic, comes to market.

1961
Ampicillin, the first synthetic penicillin, is introduced to the public.

2018
Malacidins, chemical molecules that attack bacteria in new ways, are discovered.

2002
No new antibiotics are developed or submitted for FDA approval.

2016
Pharmaceutical companies around the world sign The Declaration on Combating Antimicrobial Resistance.

1985
Carbapenem antibiotics are developed to treat multidrug-resistant bacterial infections.

1965　　1980　　1995　　2010　　2015

1970
Penicillin-resistant strains of bacteria spread around the world.

1999
Scientists confirm the emergence of pathogenic bacteria for which no known antibiotics are effective.

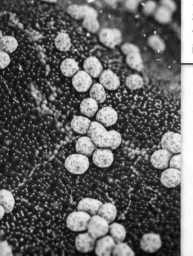

2015
Six new antibiotics receive FDA approval to treat MRSA and some multidrug resistant infections.

2017
The US FDA bans the use of antibiotics to promote growth in farm animals.

Saved by the Millions

Imagine a world in which antibiotics had never been discovered. For many people, life would be short and end in sickness and suffering. This is because antibiotics kill bacteria, which are single-celled organisms that can cause many infections and diseases. Without antibiotics, even minor injuries and sicknesses would represent an ever-present danger.

Consider, for example, a baby boy who first begins eating solid foods and accidentally ingests a piece of undercooked hamburger upon which contaminating bacteria were growing. As a result, he might develop severe diarrhea, and as more fluid leaves his body than he is able to take in, he would become dehydrated. Without antibiotics to stop the growth of bacteria in the boy's body, doctors could do little but offer supportive care and try to replace his lost fluids. Despite the best medical efforts, the baby would likely die.

Or consider a little girl, riding her bicycle, who takes a spill and skins her knee. Her mother would carefully wash the cut to try to prevent germs from getting into the wound, but there would be no antibiotic ointment to apply to the wound. Perhaps a few bacteria from the road where she fell are already inside the scrape. As hours pass, the bacteria multiply and cause an infection. Maybe the infection would clear on its own as the girl's body successfully fights off the infection, but maybe the infection would worsen. Eventually the bacterial infection might work its way into the child's bloodstream, spread through her body, and kill her.

In addition to accidental exposure to bacteria, there are many infectious diseases that are caused by bacteria—and without antibiotics, these diseases would have serious consequences. Strep throat, for example, is caused by the streptococcus bacterium. In most cases the sore throat and fever associated with this illness clear up in about a week. In some cases, however, strep throat can lead to scarlet fever, an illness that can be deadly for children and adults. In other cases strep throat might lead to rheumatic fever, which causes permanent heart damage and for which there is no treatment. Bacteria can also cause meningitis and pneumonia, diseases from which some people might recover but many others would die.

Before Antibiotics

Before antibiotics were discovered, severe illness and death from diseases and infection were common, and people tended to fear all germs that could cause sickness. *Washington Post* science editor Laura Helmuth explains: "The vast majority of deaths before the mid-20th century were caused by microbes— bacteria, amoebas, protozoans, or viruses that ruled the Earth and to a lesser extent still do."[1] Bacterial diseases were particularly serious. Millions of people died every year around the world because of these infections, and life expectancy— even in developed countries—was only forty-seven years, in part because so many children died during the first five years of life. Compare this to life expectancy in 2017, which according to the Centers for Disease Control and Prevention (CDC) averaged 78.8 years in the

> "The vast majority of deaths before the mid-20th century were caused by microbes."[1]
>
> —Laura Helmuth, *Washington Post* Science Editor

In a world without antibiotics, a scraped knee that becomes infected after a bicycle fall could lead to a more serious infection and possibly death. Antibiotics kill the bacteria that cause many harmful infections and diseases.

United States. Before antibiotics, streptococcus bacteria caused half of all deaths, and staphylococcus (staph) infections were fatal 80 percent of the time that bacteria infected a wound.

Journalist and science writer Maryn McKenna describes the death of her great-uncle Joe in 1938. Joe was a firefighter in New York City, thirty years old and recently married. One day at work a heavy hose nozzle fell on him, bruising and scraping his skin. One of the scrapes became infected. McKenna writes,

> After a few days, he developed an ache in one shoulder; two days later, a fever. His wife and the neighborhood doctor struggled for two weeks to take care of him, then flagged down a taxi and drove him fifteen miles to the hospital in my grandparents' town. He was there one more week, shaking with chills and muttering through hallucinations, and then sinking into a coma as his organs failed.[2]

Nothing anyone did could save Joe from the bacteria that ravaged his body. His life was cut short, any children he might have had were never born, and he became just one more person killed by an ordinary, seemingly trivial wound that bacteria invaded.

Alive Because of Antibiotics

If Joe McKenna's accident had happened just five years later, he likely would have lived a long and healthy life. By then antibiotics would have been available. Indeed this is antibiotics' greatest impact on the world—the millions of lives they have saved. By some scientific estimates, 75 percent of the world's population would not be alive today without antibiotics. Either these people would have died from bacterial infections or their ancestors would have died long before they ever could have been born. Antibiotics truly changed the world for humankind.

War with Germs

Throughout most of human history, no one had any idea that illnesses and infections could be caused by germs. No one even knew that the microscopic world existed until Dutch scientist Antonie Van Leeuwenhoek invented a microscope that had the power to see it. In 1674 Leeuwenhoek discovered single-celled organisms in a drop of pond water. Then, in 1683, he examined a sample of saliva under his microscope and saw that it was teeming with life. He became the first person in the world to observe and describe bacteria. He wrote of his discovery, "I then most always saw with great wonder, that in the said matter there were many very little living animalcules, very prettily a-moving."[3] The existence of microorganisms stunned the scientific world, but no one imagined that Leeuwenhoek's "animalcules" had anything to do with people or disease. That understanding would come much later.

Until the nineteenth century, the medical and scientific communities had no ability to combat infectious diseases and had little understanding of how and why diseases were contagious, spreading from person to person. Great epidemics of sickness such as plague, typhus, cholera, dysentery, and tuberculosis—all caused by infecting bacteria—ravaged whole communities and even countries. Soldiers died of infected wounds and diseases by the thousands. Everyone lived in fear of disease. Most ordinary people simply believed such epidemics were God's will, and the best theory offered by science was that bad or poisonous air caused disease and infection. But as time passed, microscopes were improved, scientists studied microorganisms, and the intersection of the human and microbial worlds became increasingly clear.

Germ Theory

Between 1857 and 1878, French chemist Louis Pasteur developed and refined what came to be known as "the germ theory of disease."[4] It states that many specific diseases are caused by specific microorganisms, or microbes, that invade the body.

Pasteur was the first human being to discover the rod-shaped bacteria that cause anthrax in cattle. He found the bacteria that caused diseases that killed silkworms (and saved France's silk industry) and the bacteria that caused deadly chicken cholera (not the same as human cholera). He discovered that bacteria could be weakened, or attenuated, and made harmless by various methods, such as heating them, exposing them to oxygen, or treating them with certain chemicals.

"I then most always saw with great wonder, that in the said matter there were many very little living animalcules, very prettily a-moving."[3]

—Dutch scientist Antonie Van Leeuwenhoek

When Pasteur injected these attenuated bacteria into animals, he discovered that the animals remained healthy and also that they did not get sick when exposed to the strong, disease-causing bacteria at a later time. Although he did not know exactly why, the animals' immune systems had developed antibodies to the weak, harmless bacteria that protected them in all further exposures to that disease.

This is the definition of a vaccine. Vaccines work by stimulating the immune system, which is the body's defense against foreign invaders and germs. The immune system attacks these microbes

French chemist Louis Pasteur works in his laboratory. Pasteur developed and refined human understanding of the connection between germs and disease.

by making antibodies that mark foreign organisms and chemically signal the immune system to destroy them. Once formed, antibodies to a specific microbe remain in the body, ready to attack quickly should that same microbe ever invade again. Vaccines protect against disease before a person or animal is exposed to it. With his attenuated bacteria, Pasteur developed vaccines for several animal diseases.

The germ theory of disease was not immediately accepted by the medical world. Pasteur vehemently and tirelessly argued, lectured, wrote papers, and insisted that diseases are caused by microbes, despite widespread disbelief. As the French newspaper *La Presse* editorialized in 1860, "The world into which you [Pasteur] wish to take us is really too fantastic."[5] Gradually, however, the scientific evidence that supported the germ theory of disease could not be ignored.

Bacteria Are Truly the Enemy

Joseph Lister, an English surgeon, read one of Pasteur's papers and applied the theory to the problem of infections after surgery. At that time more than 50 percent of all surgeries resulted in infections and death. Using his microscope, Lister determined that bacteria appeared in surgical wounds, and he developed the concept of antiseptics. He discovered that a chemical compound known as carbolic acid would kill bacteria. He began using a system that involved spraying carbolic acid in the air in his operating room, on his hands, and on the patient, both before and after surgery, in order to prevent infection. Between 1865 and 1867, as Lister put germ theory into practice in his hospital, the surgical death rate dropped to 15 percent. In later years, Lister wrote to Pasteur, "Permit me to thank you cordially for having shown me the truth of the theory of germs."[6]

During the 1870s German physician and microbiologist Robert Koch took germ theory a step further. He used rigorous laboratory analysis to identify specific bacteria and prove that they were the causes of several dreaded diseases, including tuberculosis. He also developed a way to use dye to stain bacteria so they could be seen using a microscope. He discovered that bacteria—but not any surrounding tissues—absorbed certain kinds of dyes, making it possible to identify different kinds of bacteria. Through these techniques Koch basically proved that the germ theory of disease was correct.

First Battles Against Bacteria

Identifying the bacteria that caused a disease did not automatically mean conquering that disease. However, the medical world and the general public did learn a great deal about how to prevent and avoid infections. By the beginning of the twentieth century, doctors worked to maintain sterile conditions in hospitals and surgeries. Ordinary people learned about the importance of cleanliness in their homes, in preparing their food, and in caring for wounds so as to protect themselves from becoming contaminated with germs they could not see. Sick people were isolated, or quarantined, so that they could not spread their infections to others. Vaccines were available that protected people from some infectious diseases. Still, once an infection took hold, there was no way to treat it.

One clue regarding how to treat infections came from Koch's discovery that bacteria absorbed dyes that other tissues were impervious to. What if there was a dye that was not only absorbed by bacteria but poisonous to them? Such a drug could kill the microbes but leave human tissue unharmed. In 1909 German scientist Paul Ehrlich discovered such a chemical compound that effectively killed the bacterium that causes syphilis. At that time the sexually transmitted disease disabled and killed many thousands of people each year, so the medicine—called Salvarsan—was a tremendous benefit. It did not, however, have any effect on other types of bacteria.

Then, during the early 1930s, German chemist Gerhard Domagk discovered a different class of dyes that could inhibit the growth of bacteria. These sulfonamides, as they came to be known, did not kill bacteria, but they did prevent them from reproducing. This action slowed the growth of bacterial infections so that in some cases the body's own immune system could more easily fight off the infection.

On the basis of these successes, scientists theorized that it should be possible to find a chemical that killed bacteria but was not toxic to people. However, finding such a drug proved extremely difficult. Most chemicals that killed bacteria also killed human cells. Many researchers abandoned the attempt as fruitless, but British physician and researcher Alexander Fleming did not. He believed there had to be a way to fight bacteria inside the body. Inspired by Ehrlich's success with Salvarsan, Fleming spent countless hours in his laboratory, growing dishes of many kinds of bacteria and searching for chemicals that could kill them. For a long time he was unsuccessful.

Support the Troops

One example of the impact of penicillin comes from the differences in deaths from bacterial infections in the two world wars. During World War I deaths from bacterial pneumonia in solders averaged 18 percent. In World War II, however, this death rate dropped to less than 1 percent. In large part, the lives of wounded soldiers were saved by the patriotism and determination of drug company scientists and employees who worked feverishly to produce enough penicillin for the troops. The director of the US government's penicillin program, Albert Elder, wrote to the drug companies, "You are urged to impress upon every worker in your plant that penicillin produced today will be saving the life of someone in a few days or curing the disease of someone now incapacitated. Put up slogans in your plant! Place notices in pay envelopes! Create an enthusiasm for the job down to the lowest worker in your plant."

One poster, for instance, read, "Penicillin, The New Life-Saving Drug, Saves Soldiers' Lives!" Other posters informed the construction workers building new penicillin manufacturing plants that the faster the building was completed, the more soldiers would be saved by the drug. Everyone was doing their part in the war effort, and by 1944 there was enough penicillin available to treat every wounded soldier who needed it.

Quoted in American Chemical Society International Historic Chemical Landmarks, "Discovery and Development of Penicillin." www.acs.org.

Quoted in Roswell Quinn, MD, PhD, "Rethinking Antibiotic Research and Development: World War II and the Penicillin Collaborative," *American Journal of Public Health* vol. 103, no. 3 (2013): 426–34. www.ncbi.nlm.nih.gov.

Alexander Fleming and Penicillin

Fleming was a respected and capable physician and researcher, but neatness was not his strength. He seemed to not want to be bothered with cleaning up. Old, abandoned experiments sat around for weeks. His lab sink was always full of the dirty petri dishes in which he had grown bacteria. Other petri dishes and samples of chemicals and microorganisms might be left on shelves and windowsills for days on end. In part, Fleming saw his disorganized habits as an asset. He once explained to an assistant that it was not beneficial to be too neat. He thought that perhaps something unusual or interesting might occur in an old petri dish sample—and he was right.

One morning in August 1928, Fleming returned to his lab after a two-week vacation in Scotland. Dozens of different petri dishes containing strains of staph bacteria sat around the lab, just as he had left them before starting his vacation. Most were ruined and worthless. They had sat in the open air, unprotected from any substance that might fall on and contaminate them. The samples needed to be discarded and the petri dishes cleaned for future use. As Fleming was talking with a coworker, he picked up one of the dishes of bacteria and saw that it had been contaminated by a mold. That was a typical event in any lab, but this mold was not typical at all. Fleming stopped talking and stared at the petri dish. In the area around the growing mold, the dish was clear of bacteria. Something in one living organism (the mold) was preventing the growth of another organism (the colony of staph bacteria) and killing it. "That's funny,"[7] Fleming famously commented.

A handwritten note signed by Alexander Fleming identifies the capsule on the left as containing the original penicillin mold from which he discovered the drug penicillin. Fleming spent countless hours on the work that eventually yielded his miraculous discovery.

Fleming carefully scraped out some of the mold and put it into a small tube of broth to keep it alive. He wanted to study this unusual mold and its chemical properties. As the weeks passed, he discovered that some chemical substance produced by the mold killed staphylococcus bacteria, streptococcus bacteria, and the bacteria that cause diphtheria. He was not a chemist, but he tried to dissolve out the specific chemical that was at work. He grew the mold in a broth that turned yellow after a few days. He filtered the broth, diluted it, and found that even the weakest solution still killed staph bacteria. It was many hundred times more powerful than the strongest antiseptic then known. Just as important, it had no effect on the white blood cells that fight infection in the human body. It harmed only bacteria. Fleming later wrote of his discovery, "It was the first substance I had ever tested which was more antibacterial than it was antileukocytic [harmful to white blood cells] and it was this especially which convinced me that some day when it could be concentrated and rendered more stable it would be used for treatment of infection."[8]

Fleming had discovered penicillin, the world's first antibiotic. An antibiotic is a substance produced by one microorganism that destroys other microorganisms. It was produced by a rare species of fungi from the genus *Penicillium*, but Fleming could not even identify it accurately, and he could not purify the chemical substance it produced. Even more problematic, the substance was unstable, meaning it easily decomposed in about two weeks. Fleming could not develop a medicine from it by himself and therefore tried to interest other scientists in his discovery. He wrote papers about his mold, gave talks about it to scientific gatherings, and sent samples of the mold to various research laboratories. No one paid any attention to him.

It Takes a Team

Ten years passed. Then, in 1938, Howard Florey, Ernst Chain, and Norman Heatley at the University of Oxford were studying bacteria. They discovered one of Fleming's old papers about penicillin and further realized that the university had stored an old sample

The Cocoanut Grove Fire

On November 28, 1942, a deadly fire broke out in the Cocoanut Grove nightclub in Boston, Massachusetts. More than one thousand people were packed into the building, where fire exit doors were locked, and only one revolving door allowed for any escape. The fire flashed through the whole place in minutes, killing 492 people and injuring more than 400 others. The badly burned survivors were treated at several hospitals in the Boston area. Severe burns leave patients without protection against infections by microorganisms, and many survivors subsequently died.

Thirty-nine fortunate victims, however, found themselves at Massachusetts General Hospital. Despite the fact that penicillin was prioritized for the military, Massachusetts General Hospital was able to get 32 liters of penicillin from the drug manufacturer Merck & Company. On December 12, two chemists from Merck, under police escort, rushed the drug from Rahway, New Jersey, to Massachusetts General Hospital. It was the world's first large-scale civilian use of penicillin, and it was spectacularly successful. Of the one hundred victims treated at another hospital, Boston City Hospital, one-third died over the next month. At Massachusetts General Hospital, however, every victim survived.

Fleming had sent there. The team was interested. They identified the mold sample as a strain of *Penicillium notatum* and set about researching the possibility of actually making a medicine of penicillin. They worked out a method of purifying the unstable penicillin from a broth of the mold, essentially evaporating the mold juice over and over, freeze-drying it. It took many gallons of mold juice to get a fingernail's amount of penicillin. Even that small amount was not completely pure, but it proved its worth: when injected into mice, it did not harm them at all, and when injected into mice infected with three different disease bacteria, it cured them.

In 1940 the team reported their findings in the medical journal the *Lancet.* Fleming read the article and was thrilled. He visited Oxford to meet the team and express his thankfulness and pleasure at their success. Next, the team tried to talk British pharmaceutical companies into purifying penicillin, because they could produce so little by themselves. What they really needed was a whole factory producing it so as to have enough to try treating people with it. However, every drug company refused. By this time World War II was raging in Europe, and all of Great Britain's companies were devoted to producing proven medicines or other war materials. The Oxford team continued their own efforts and made enough penicillin to give to one human being. He was policeman Albert Alexander, who was dying from a staph infection that took hold when he was scratched by a rose thorn. At first the dying man improved dramatically, but they did not have enough penicillin to kill all the bacteria. When the supply of penicillin ran out, the infection raged again, and the man died.

Manufacturing a Miracle

The team turned to the United States for help. With funding from the US government, several American drug companies agreed to attempt large-scale production of penicillin, and in Peoria, Illinois,

Supplies of penicillin were initially earmarked for soldiers. Within a short time, drug companies began mass production (pictured) of the new wonder drug.

with the help of the US Department of Agriculture, a broth made of corn steep liquor (a waste product from manufacturing cornstarch) was discovered to produce amazing amounts of penicillin when *Penicillium notatum* and other *Penicillium* strains were fermented in it. By 1942, when the United States was deep into World War II, the US government took over the manufacture of penicillin and poured unlimited funding into it as critical to the war effort. Anything that could reduce the casualties caused by infections was seen as essential to winning the war.

The first person saved by penicillin was not a soldier. She was Anne Miller, a Connecticut woman who in 1942 was dying of septicemia, or blood poisoning, caused by strep bacteria. Her doctor was treating another patient who was friends with Florey (the Oxford scientist) and connected Florey and the doctor. Florey gave the doctor about a tablespoon of penicillin. It was almost half the penicillin then available in the United States. Within a day of beginning treatment Miller's fever disappeared, and by the time she completed the course of penicillin, she was cured.

As it became clear that the drug was a lifesaver, penicillin production efforts increased. Deep corn steep liquor fermentation tanks were built to grow and purify penicillin. At first the supply of penicillin was earmarked for soldiers in military hospitals, and historians estimate that thousands of wounded soldiers were saved. Soon, however, the drug companies were pouring out enough penicillin for everyone. By the end of 1943 drug companies had produced 21 billion units of penicillin. In 1944 that amount increased to 1.6 trillion units, and in 1945 it was 6.8 trillion units. Penicillin was a "wonder drug," and freely available to all by war's end. In the journal *P&S*, science writer Eric Oatman argues, "Of all the weapons developed during World War II, penicillin was probably the most important."[9] Humanity's war against germs had officially begun.

> "Of all the weapons developed during World War II, penicillin was probably the most important."[9]
>
> —Eric Oatman, science writer

CHAPTER 2

The Golden Age of Antibiotics

Penicillin was the first antibiotic, but it was far from the last. Its discovery ushered in the golden age of antibiotics, which lasted roughly from the 1940s through the 1960s. Many more antibiotics were discovered and synthesized as the medical world realized that if one microbe produced a bacteria-killing chemical, there must be more that could kill other bacteria. Infections that were once fatal could be cured in just a few days. Humankind was determined to win the war against infectious bacteria.

A Diverse Bacterial World

Penicillin was a wonder drug that cured infections caused by staphylococcus and streptococcus. It could also kill the genus of bacteria known as listeria, which was often the cause of food poisoning. But penicillin was not perfect. The bacterial world may be microscopic, but it is vast and complex. Bacteria are living, extremely diverse, single-celled organisms, and countless numbers of them exist on Earth. Even though scientists estimate there are less than one hundred bacterial species that cause disease in humans, those bacteria have different characteristics, structures, and capabilities.

One major difference among bacteria is the kind of cell wall they possess. Bacteria with thick cell walls are called gram-positive bacteria, while those with thin cell walls that are protected by outer membranes are gram-negative bacteria. Penicillin is effective only against gram-positive bacteria. It cannot penetrate the membrane surrounding gram-negative bacteria, destroy the cell wall, and thus kill the bacteria. Staphylococcus and streptococcus bacteria are gram positive; so are listeria, the bacterium that causes diphtheria, and two species of clostridium, bacteria that cause tetanus and botulism. Gram-negative bacteria, however, cause several deadly diseases, too, and they could not yet be cured.

Medical scientists were not discouraged by penicillin's limitations. On the contrary, they were galvanized by the implications of penicillin's success and the likelihood of discovering more antibiotics. In their natural environment, microorganisms produce chemical substances to destroy competing microorganisms, and thereby protect their ability to reproduce, form colonies, and maintain a habitat with sufficient nutrients and water. A single teaspoon of average, ordinary soil can contain millions of microbes of thousands of species. The inspiring speculation was that many other microbes existed with antibiotic properties that could be used to fight disease.

Selman Waksman's Actinomycetes

Selman Waksman, a Ukrainian immigrant to the United States and soil microbiologist, was certain that he could find antibiotics that were more effective than penicillin. In his laboratory at Rutgers University in New Jersey, Waksman and his team of graduate students studied the effects of microorganisms on the health of soil. They were particularly studying actinomycetes, a large group of bacteria with many species. The research team had already discovered that about half of all the species of actinomycetes could inhibit the growth of other bacteria and fungi. When Waksman learned about the success of penicillin and its mass production in the early 1940s, he said to his research team, "Drop everything; see what these English have done with a mould. I know the actinomycetes will do better."[10]

Selman Waksman (center) works with other researchers in his lab. Waksman, who was a soil microbiologist, was confident he could find antibiotics that performed better than penicillin.

In the first deliberate effort to find a new antibiotic, Waksman and his team grew cultures of actinomycetes of different species, one by one, and then added pathogenic (disease-causing) bacteria to each culture to see what would happen. Then in 1944, Waksman's team member, student Albert Schatz, grew a strain of actinomycetes known as *Streptomyces griseus*. He tested it with several kinds of pathogenic bacteria, and it seemed to strongly inhibit bacterial growth. He was able to isolate the chemical substance that was at work. It was named streptomycin, and amazingly, it worked to destroy several pathogenic bacteria that penicillin could not. It killed the gram-negative bacteria that cause urinary infections, some kinds of pneumonia, and a form of food poisoning caused by salmonella bacteria. It also worked against some gram-positive bacteria.

Most important, however, was the fact that streptomycin killed the bacterium that causes tuberculosis, or TB. At that time TB was known as the White Plague (because its victims had a

Scientist Heroes

The discoverers of antibiotics became heroes to the general public and espe-cially to parents whose children were saved by the new drugs. During his life-time Selman Waksman received hundreds of letters from people thanking him for saving the lives of their children by discovering streptomycin.

One parent, for instance, wrote to Waksman that streptomycin was "a magi-cal name because the doctors tell me that this is the drug that was responsible for saving my baby's life." Such drugs had never existed before or even been imagined. Waksman was extremely moved by the expressions of gratitude he received and by seeing for himself the results of his work. He once asked, "How can I describe the impressions left upon me by the first sight of a child…who had been saved from certain death by the use of a drug in the discovery of which I had played but a humble part?"

Quoted in Nancy Tomes, *The Gospel of Germs: Men, Women, and the Microbe in American Life.* Cambridge, MA: Harvard University Press, 1998, p. 254.

pale appearance), and it killed millions around the world every year. *Mycobacterium tuberculosis*, the bacterium that causes TB, is a strange bacterium with odd cell walls. It is neither gram negative nor gram positive, and its walls have characteristics of both types. Penicillin had no effect on the bacteria, but strepto-mycin did, and it was not toxic to humans. Once streptomycin was mass produced and brought to market in the late 1940s, TB was a killer no more.

Waksman gained fame and honor (including the Nobel Prize) for the discovery of streptomycin and for his strategy for identifying and testing the antibiotic properties of microorgan-isms. Schatz, although only a graduate student at the time, also receives credit today for his part in the discovery. Waksman, however, became known as the "Father of Antibiotics,"[11] and was the first scientist to suggest the name "antibiotics" for the natural substances produced by microorganisms that destroy bacteria.

Antibiotics Everywhere

With the overwhelming success of penicillin and streptomycin, drug companies and researchers began an intense search all over the world for soil microbes that had antibiotic properties and could be turned into medicines. No one knew how many thousands of undiscovered, unidentified strains of microorganisms there might be or how they might be useful to humankind. Professor George Wong of the University of Hawaii explains: "The pharmaceutical companies . . . began by begging airline pilots, missionaries, traveling salesmen, vacationers and soldiers to bring back soil samples. It was in this way that Chas. Pfizer & Co., which would become one of the largest drug manufacturers, built up a culture library of more than 20,000 samples."[12]

Pfizer was not the only pharmaceutical company begging for soil samples. The drug company Eli Lilly asked Christian missionaries to send a soil sample from every place they visited. As the samples arrived at Eli Lilly's research labs, scientists isolated and grew the different strains of microorganisms in separate nutrient dishes and then tested each microbe for antibiotic activity. Many microorganisms with antibiotic properties were found, but few were useful. They turned out to be highly toxic to animals and people, as well as bacteria.

> "The pharmaceutical companies [begged] airline pilots, missionaries, traveling salesmen, vacationers and soldiers to bring back soil samples. It was in this way that Chas. Pfizer & Co., . . . built up a culture library of more than 20,000 samples."[12]
>
> —Professor George Wong, University of Hawaii

One soil sample that a missionary sent from the jungles of Borneo, however, yielded a valuable find. It was evaluated by Eli Lilly chemist E.C. Kornfield, who succeeded in isolating and growing a bacterium from it. The bacterium produced a substance that was toxic to most gram-positive bacteria, including those that cause staph infections and gonorrhea (a sexually transmitted disease). In experiments with animals and then people, the substance proved nontoxic and could cure even serious infections that were too strong for penicillin to eradicate completely. The compound became the antibiotic vancomycin and was made available to the public in 1958.

In 1947, at another pharmaceutical company, Parke-Davis, researchers discovered a strain of the *Streptomyces griseus* actinomycete that was slightly different from the one Waksman used to produce streptomycin. This strain came from a soil sample from a farming field in Venezuela, and it was active against both gram-positive and gram-negative bacteria. Coincidentally lab researchers at the University of Illinois found the same substance in a sample from a compost heap in Urbana. The substance became the antibiotic chloramphenicol. It worked to kill salmonella bacteria and, most importantly, could destroy the unusual bacteria known

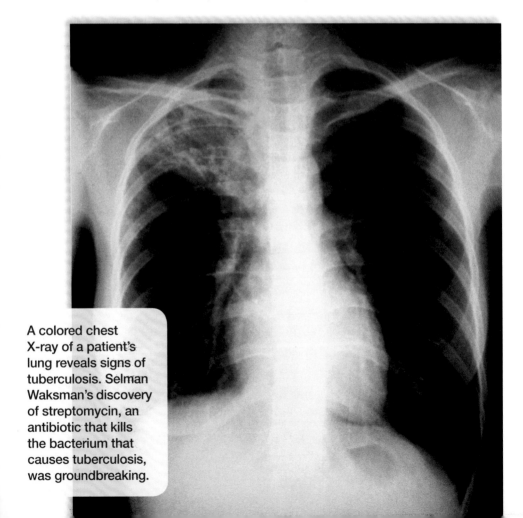

A colored chest X-ray of a patient's lung reveals signs of tuberculosis. Selman Waksman's discovery of streptomycin, an antibiotic that kills the bacterium that causes tuberculosis, was groundbreaking.

as rickettsia. This type of bacteria causes diseases such as Rocky Mountain spotted fever and typhus (a serious, often fatal fever spread by lice, fleas, and ticks that carry the bacteria).

Most antibiotics were discovered in soil samples, but the antibiotic fungus known as *Cephalosporium acremonium* was discovered in sewage. In Italy, during World War II, researcher Giuseppe Brotzu was trying to understand why his city's untreated sewage released into the sea was not making people sick with typhoid fever. Sewage is loaded with nutrients in which microorganisms flourish, including the bacteria that cause typhoid. Yet very few people swimming in the sea and sometimes swallowing the water came down with typhoid. People did not even develop skin rashes from bacteria in the water.

As Brotzu analyzed different samples of sea water, he found that the water contained the *Cephalosporium acremonium* fungus that was responsible for protecting the swimmers and killing pathogenic bacteria. Brotzu was unable to interest anyone in his country in his discovery, so in 1945 he sent a sample of his fungus to Howard Florey at Oxford. Researchers at Florey's lab, including biochemist E.P. Abraham, studied the fungus and were able to isolate the chemical substance that became the antibiotic cephalosporin in 1962. Cephalosporins are similar to penicillin and can be used for skin and ear infections, some forms of pneumonia, and meningitis.

Shifting Research Strategies

As drug companies continued their searches, thousands of antibiotics were discovered that worked in different ways and could be used to treat different infections. Where one antibiotic had a weak effect, another seemed to work easily. Some had to be injected; some could be taken orally, and some worked topically, such as bacitracin and Neosporin. Antibiotics were also found that could treat plant diseases, not just infections in people and animals. Still only about 5 percent of the antibiotics discovered were useful; the rest were lethal to the person, animal, or plant

The common cat flea (shown in this colored scanning electron micrograph) is associated with the disease typhus. Infected fleas can transmit the disease to humans.

being treated, as well as to bacteria. Today there are about one hundred antibiotics available for medical use.

As the years passed, scientists made extensive progress in understanding and identifying the molecular structure and chemical makeup of antibiotics. The worldwide search for soil samples was becoming less productive as the same microorganisms were found over and over in different soil samples. In addition, antibiotics often caused unwanted side effects, such as stomach upset and skin rashes. Some people could not tolerate them at all. A new kind of research developed in an effort to produce improved antibiotics and manufacture them more efficiently. Scientists learned to chemically alter existing antibiotics and to synthesize the substances in the lab.

Modifying Antibiotics

Tetracycline was the first antibiotic made by chemically altering an existing natural antibiotic. It was developed by Lloyd Conover, of Pfizer. Science as a whole advanced due to Conover's experiments with antibiotics. In 1952 Pfizer was marketing two antibiotics, Aureomycin and Terramycin. Aureomycin was the first so-called broad-spectrum antibiotic ever discovered (found in a soil sample from Missouri). Both Aureomycin and Terramycin are considered broad-spectrum antibiotics because they act on a wide range of gram-positive and gram-negative bacteria. Conover and the Pfizer research department were studying the molecular structure of these antibiotics to try to understand how they stopped bacteria from growing. No one was thinking about making a *better* antibiotic. In fact, no one thought that was even possible. All scientists believed that antibiotics could come only from substances found in nature. As Conover once explained, "It was the conventional wisdom that what these wonderful molecules made by living organisms just can't be improved on."[13]

As Conover analyzed the molecules of the two antibiotics, however, he realized how very similar they are. They differ by only two atoms. Molecules can be broken down into atoms, and Conover wondered what would happen if he changed those atoms. His idea was to chemically replace the chlorine atom in Aureomycin with a hydrogen atom, and do the same with the oxygen atom in Terramycin. He would have made a completely new molecule by bonding the hydrogen atom to the rest of the antibiotic molecule. "That molecule that was then unknown," he later said, "ought to be just as good and maybe better than either Terramycin or Aureomycin."[14] Conover's experiment worked. He had invented tetracycline, which came to market in 1955. It treated more infections than any other broad-spectrum antibiotic of the time while causing fewer side effects.

Synthetic Antibiotics

Throughout the pharmaceutical industry, researchers began looking for ways to modify existing antibiotics and improve upon nature. This led them to develop synthetic antibiotics. Most of the important antibiotics in use since then have been created by altering the chemical structures of existing molecules. In 1957, at the Massachusetts Institute of Technology (MIT), John C. Sheehan developed chemically synthesized penicillin. His discovery became ampicillin. At that time, regular penicillin took months to grow in fermentation tanks and also had to be injected to be effective. In contrast, ampicillin could be taken orally, and by the early 1960s, could be chemically produced rather than grown in tanks. Drug companies next learned to synthesize many varieties of penicillin that could target specific diseases—particular penicillin formulations to efficiently destroy particular pathogenic bacteria.

Today, the synthetic antibiotics ampicillin, chemically altered cephalosporin, and modified tetracyclines are the top three most commonly prescribed antibiotics in the world. Natural antibiotics are still important, but not as necessary as they once were. In addition, synthetic penicillins, such as ampicillin and amoxicillin (also developed in the 1960s), cause far fewer allergies and side effects than penicillin originally did.

An Antibiotic for Every Need

By the 1960s so many effective and powerful antibiotics had been developed that the war against pathogenic bacteria seemed to be won. In the developed world, people no longer needed to suffer the pain, torment, and disability caused by bacterial diseases. Children with strep infections no longer ran the risk of developing rheumatic fever and permanent heart damage—antibiotics cured them before these complications ever developed. People with serious wound infections in arms or legs did not face the prospect of amputation. Instead their limbs were saved with antibiotics, and they avoided lifelong disability. Even the unusual bacteria that cause TB were conquerable.

Medical researchers had also discovered that combinations of antibiotics could eradicate the bacteria that often were unaffected by a single drug. Broad-spectrum antibiotics were so effective against so many different infectious bacteria that doctors no longer had to bother identifying the bacterium that caused a particular illness. Whether a person had an ear infection, a kidney infection, or just a high fever, a broad-spectrum antibiotic took care of the problem in just a few days.

As a result, deaths from bacterial diseases plummeted in societies throughout the developed world. In the United States, for example, approximately three hundred thousand people had died in 1930 from bacterial diseases and infections. That was 22 percent

Discovering Aureomycin

Aureomycin was discovered by botanist Benjamin Minge Duggar when he was seventy-six years old. At the time Duggar was a consultant for the drug company Lederle and was searching for new antibiotics. Penicillin and streptomycin were already in widespread use, but there were some bacterial infections that did not respond to these drugs.

Duggar analyzed a collection of thirty-five hundred mold samples from soil and found a particularly interesting one from soil on the University of Missouri campus where he was a professor of botany. The mold in the sample produced a golden colored chemical substance that seemed to be active against staph, strep, and many other kinds of bacteria. Extensive testing showed the substance to be effective against 90 percent of pathogenic bacteria and nontoxic to animals and people. Furthermore, it could be taken orally, in pills, instead of needing to be injected into the bloodstream like penicillin and streptomycin. Duggar named his new antibiotic for its golden color by combining the Latin word for gold, "aureus" with the Greek word "mykes" for fungus.

Aureomycin worked for both gram-positive and gram-negative bacteria. Within the first year of its introduction, it became popular with doctors for treating diseases such as pneumonia, eye infections, strep and staph infections, and Rocky Mountain spotted fever. It was popular with children, too, because they did not have to get shots. This medicine could be swallowed instead.

of all the deaths in that year. By 1952, however, antibiotics were in widespread use, and just ninety-five thousand people died of bacterial disease—only 6 percent of deaths in that year. Experts estimate that five to ten years have been added to the life expectancy of US citizens because of the availability of antibiotics.

If one antibiotic did not work for an individual, or if he or she experienced bad side effects from that drug, another could be substituted that solved the problem. If one kind of bacteria did not respond to an antibiotic treatment, another, more powerful antibiotic would work. The general public lost its fear of infectious disease. The medical world believed that pathogenic bacteria had been conquered.

Medical doctor and infectious disease specialist Robert P. Gaynes remembers how confident doctors felt about curing bacterial infections by the time he entered the profession in 1978. He explains, "I entered the specialty at a time when it was believed that medical science had nearly done it all—that there would be little left to do since we had such powerful agents for treating and curing infectious diseases."[15] Gaynes was not even sure that his specialty in infectious disease would be needed anymore in the future. Perhaps, said some medical experts of the time, bacterial diseases would disappear within the next ten years. Perhaps the only microorganisms that would be left to infect people would be viruses, fungi, and microscopic parasites. The threat from bacterial infection seemed to be gone.

"I entered the specialty at a time when it was believed that medical science had nearly done it all—that there would be little left to do since we had such powerful agents for treating and curing infectious diseases."[15]

—Robert P. Gaynes, infectious disease specialist

CHAPTER 3

The Impact of Antibiotics

Antibiotics revolutionized the human world. Their discovery not only changed the practice of medicine and medical research but also established the pharmaceutical industry, transformed agriculture, and critically impacted the relationship between the federal government and the medical world.

Specializing in Infectious Disease

Because of antibiotics' extraordinary success in conquering infectious disease, a new medical specialty came into being. Infectious disease specialists had expertise in a wide spectrum of infectious diseases, and it was their job to identify, diagnose, and treat these diseases with an appropriate dose of the correct antibiotic. By the 1960s, this specialty was needed; many contagious diseases became so rare that most doctors never saw a case of tuberculosis or typhus or diphtheria. As antibiotic use became more widespread, epidemics of these diseases had become things of the past.

As a wide variety of antibiotics became available and more popular, infectious disease specialists began to see a problem. Now any doctor could prescribe an antibiotic for whatever reason. This meant that antibiotics were often prescribed whether or not an illness was caused by bacteria. It meant that new, expensive antibiotics that had never been proved to be effective or worthwhile were frequently prescribed. Infectious disease specialists found themselves becoming guardians of public health. They were instrumental in protecting people from less desirable antibiotics promoted by sometimes overzealous drug companies. Some of the specialists became reformers who fought to change how antibiotics were developed and prescribed. The modern Food and Drug Administration (FDA) was given the authority it has today in large part because of their efforts.

Too Many Untested Antibiotics

One of these reformers was Maxwell Finland, an infectious disease specialist and scientist at Boston City Hospital. Finland believed that a good medical doctor should be both a scientist and a skeptic and rely only on those drugs that proved to be effective and beneficial. During the 1950s he became concerned that this philosophy was being ignored. Pharmaceutical companies had begun marketing their own, patented antibiotics to doctors as better choices than the older antibiotics, penicillin and streptomycin. No drug company owned the exclusive rights to market those two drugs, and so they were not very profitable. Patented antibiotics were profitable, and pharmaceutical companies aggressively marketed their own broad-spectrum antibiotics to physicians as much more versatile than penicillin and streptomycin, and as much better than another company's antibiotic. Each drug company claimed that its antibiotic was the best.

For overworked doctors, accepting the drug companies' marketing claims was easier than being skeptical. They could prescribe these broad-spectrum antibiotics, and usually their patients got better. Perhaps the patients did not need a broad-spectrum antibiotic and would have done fine just with penicillin or streptomycin. Perhaps these patients would have gotten better without any antibiotic. Neither doctors nor drug companies seemed to question the value of or need for the expensive prescriptions. By

1956 broad-spectrum antibiotics accounted for the majority of all drug sales nationwide. Finland and others worried about excessive dependence on broad-spectrum antibiotics that were sold as necessary and best with no scientific proof.

Then drug companies began combining their antibiotics into fixed-dose combinations. For instance, Pfizer developed Sigmamycin, a combination of tetracycline and another antibiotic called oleandomycin. As with other combination drugs, it was supposed to offer the powerful action of both medicines. It was claimed that such combinations increased the effect of both antibiotics, making them work better together than each would alone.

Finland looked at these claims with serious skepticism. He knew that some antibiotics could work well together, but some were antagonistic—that is, some antibiotics actually inhibited the effects of other antibiotics by attacking them. In addition, Finland believed antibiotics were being abused, overprescribed, and causing more side effects in patients. Too many physicians were prescribing such antibiotics without ever diagnosing the specific microbe responsible for the patient's illness. The risk was that bacteria might grow accustomed to them and develop defenses.

Finland looked for scientific evidence that drugs like Sigmamycin were safe and effective but could not find any. By the late 1950s drug companies were marketing sixty-one combination drugs to physicians, with little proof that they were beneficial. They were advertised to doctors in medical journals and through drug company salespeople, but proof of their value was lacking. Busy doctors just assumed the combination antibiotics were best for their patients and worth the cost. Based on the drug companies' recommendations, they prescribed antibiotics for almost every ailment, even viral illnesses that were unaffected by antibiotics, such as the common cold.

In 1957, Finland, with the support of eighteen other infectious disease specialists, wrote a paper in which he argued, "Much of the clinical information presented [about combination antibiotics] had the sound of testimonials rather than carefully collected and adequately documented scientific data."[16] Testimonials are not scientific evidence. They are just reports from doctors or patients that claim they were cured after they used the drug. There is no way to prove the truth or falsity of the claims.

Empowering the Modern FDA

The infectious disease reformers began campaigning for the use of clinical trials to establish the safety and efficacy of new drugs. Clinical trials are a series of tightly controlled scientific studies of medications or treatments. Usually they involve testing the proposed treatment in groups of volunteers, half of whom receive the medicine and half of whom do not. Comparing the groups' results yields evidence of the treatment's effectiveness. Almost no one was performing clinical trials of different combinations of antibiotics in the late 1950s, however.

> "Much of the clinical information presented [about combination antibiotics] had the sound of testimonials rather than carefully collected and adequately documented scientific data."[16]
>
> —Maxwell Finland, infectious disease specialist

Concerned infectious disease specialists urged doctors to demand independent scientific studies that reliably demonstrated the value of drugs and to reject testimonials provided by drug companies when they chose what to prescribe a patient. Finland conducted his own studies of combination antibiotics and found them to be no more beneficial than each component antibiotic would have been on its own. Finland wrote a letter about his concerns to Selman Waksman saying, "Something drastic will have to be done to stop this before long."[17]

The controversy gained public attention as investigative reporters described the sometimes false testimonials presented by drug companies about their products. In 1959 John Lear, the science editor for the Saturday Review magazine, wrote an article titled "Taking the Miracle Out of the Miracle Drugs." The article shocked readers with its description of antibiotics' overuse and the "massive advertising pressure"[18] on doctors to prescribe them. That same year, the US Senate held hearings on the subject of antibiotic overuse, pharmaceutical marketing of unproven antibiotics, and the role of the FDA in protecting the public. At the hearings, infectious disease specialist Louis Lasagna, one of the antibiotic reformers, testified that it was "shocking that experimental drugs are subject to no FDA regulation of any sort before patients receive them."[19] The FDA had been authorized to evaluate the safety of drugs as far back as 1938, but it did not play any role in determining drug efficacy. In other words, it could demand proof that a drug would not harm any of its users, but even a worthless drug could be marketed, so long as it was safe.

The 1959 Senate hearings led to laws passed in 1962 that authorized and empowered the FDA to regulate the introduction of new drugs. Drugs were approved only after controlled studies and clinical trials demonstrated both safety and efficacy. It took several years and a disaster with another drug—thalidomide, which caused severe birth defects when pregnant women took

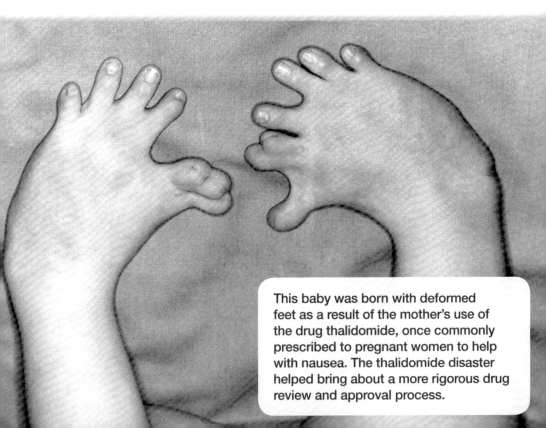

This baby was born with deformed feet as a result of the mother's use of the drug thalidomide, once commonly prescribed to pregnant women to help with nausea. The thalidomide disaster helped bring about a more rigorous drug review and approval process.

it—but by 1970, all combination antibiotics had been decertified by the FDA and pulled from the market. Writing in the *FDA Consumer Magazine*, Michelle Meadows explains, "Today, the drug review process in the United States is recognized worldwide as the gold standard. Drugs must undergo a rigorous evaluation of safety, quality, and effectiveness before they can be sold."[20] The efforts of infectious disease specialists to ensure the efficacy of antibiotics changed the drug approval system for all medicine in the United States.

Establishing the Pharmaceutical Industry

Pharmaceutical companies had resisted FDA regulations as impractical, but in the end they were not harmed by the new regulations. As a matter of fact, the modern pharmaceutical industry owes its existence to antibiotics. The drive to produce enough penicillin for the troops in World War II began this process. Science writer Robin Walsh explains, "The immense scale and sophistication of the penicillin development effort marked a new era for the way the pharmaceutical industry developed drugs."[21] Drug companies became profitable enough (with the help of government funding) to establish expansive research and development facilities in order to discover and develop new drugs that were even more profitable, and these major drug companies grew even larger. Smaller drug companies that had not been part of the penicillin production gradually died out.

Over time, today's medical system was established, in which drugs are marketed to doctors who prescribe them to patients who buy them at pharmacies. Writing for the American Chemical Society, Arthur H. Daemmrich and Mary Ellen Bowden add, "Drug salesmanship

"The immense scale and sophistication of the penicillin development effort marked a new era for the way the pharmaceutical industry developed drugs."[21]

—Robin Walsh, science writer

Antibiotics' Impact on Social Mores

Before antibiotics, sexually transmitted diseases posed a real threat of disability and death. In many ways the dangers from diseases such as syphilis and gonorrhea may have limited people's willingness to engage in sexual behavior except in traditional circumstances, such as marriage. However once these diseases could be easily cured with antibiotics, the risk became so low that people began to think differently about sexual morality and behavior.

It may even be that antibiotics were a major cause of the sexual revolution that occurred in the 1960s. In that decade society's attitudes toward sex outside of marriage, casual sex, sex with multiple partners, and single mothers became more flexible and tolerant. With a dramatically reduced fear of disease and death, the moral strictures regarding sex were radically altered. People could embrace ideas about free love and natural sexual contact because they believed no harm would come to them (this was before the advent of the AIDS virus, which decidedly changed that view). Of course no one can prove that antibiotics led to the swinging sixties, but an economist named Andrew Francis performed a mathematical analysis that demonstrated a rise in "risky nontraditional sex" directly coinciding with the fall of syphilis infections and deaths in the United States.

Quoted in Kate Shaw Yoshida, "Did Antibiotics Spur the Sexual Revolution?," *Ars Technica*, February 1, 2013. https://arstechnica.com.

was transformed into a professional service that educated physicians about new therapeutic options."[22] Both the medical community and the federal government still rely on the pharmaceutical industry to research new drugs and conduct clinical trials. Prescription drugs continue to be the most profitable components of any drug company's products.

An Expanded Drug Industry

The profit motive for producing new drugs is not necessarily bad. Profits give the pharmaceutical industry the means to support their research facilities and discover important drugs. As

Professor George Wong points out, "It is of interest to note that during the early development of antibiotics, the iron curtain countries [former communist countries of Eastern Europe and the Soviet Union] did not play a role in antibiotic development, leaving one to assume that the capitalistic system must . . . in some way serve as a stimulus for their development."[23] In addition, despite the need for government regulation and oversight, the pharmaceutical industry has always been concerned about the greater good. George Merck, then-president of Merck & Company, said in 1950, "We try never to forget that medicine is for the people. It is not for the profits. The profits follow."[24]

The profits earned from antibiotics, as well as the technologies and laboratory techniques developed, led to drug discoveries in many areas of medicine. For example, one fungal antibiotic called griseofulvin was discovered to be effective in fighting fungal infections as well as bacteria. It can be used for infections of the skin, nails, and hair, such as ringworm (which is not a worm

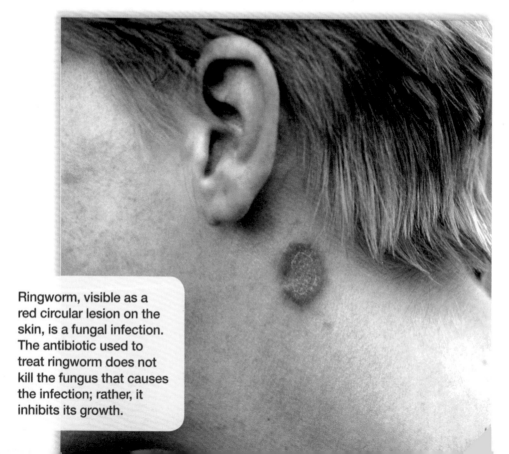

Ringworm, visible as a red circular lesion on the skin, is a fungal infection. The antibiotic used to treat ringworm does not kill the fungus that causes the infection; rather, it inhibits its growth.

but a fungus). It does not kill fungi but inhibits their growth so that new skin and nails are uninfected, and the infection slowly disappears. Another antibiotic, cilofungin, is chemically modified and partially synthetic; it features the same technology developed to synthetically produce forms of penicillin. It can kill thrush and yeast infections, both caused by fungi. Some antibiotics have been discovered that are useful for diseases caused by things other than microorganisms, such as cancer. These antibiotics are toxic, but when carefully injected into a tumor, they can kill or slow the growth of cancer cells. Still other drugs developed using antibiotic technology have proved useful in treating autoimmune diseases and producing new vaccines.

Antibiotics Transform Agriculture

Antibiotics also have had a huge impact on modern agriculture, changing the way livestock are raised and made available to the public. Indeed antibiotics have made industrialized agriculture possible. After World War II researchers began experimenting with the use of antibiotics in farm animals, first with chickens. The public wanted meat and wanted it cheap, but raising large numbers of animals cheaply was not easy for farmers. They began to raise chickens in unnatural, confined environments and barns, where the chickens had to be fed artificially instead of finding food for themselves outdoors. Feed was expensive, but when farmers switched to cheaper feed, chickens did not grow well. Adding vitamins to cheap feed helped, but the chickens still grew too slowly and were too small for farmers to make much of a profit.

Then in 1948, Thomas Jukes, a researcher for the pharmaceutical company Lederle, discovered that the company's top-selling antibiotic for people did amazing things for chickens, too. The antibiotic was Aureomycin, and in his chicken experiments, Jukes discovered that minute quantities of the antibiotic in chicken feed made the chickens grow bigger. Chickens fed Aureomycin were 50 percent bigger than those fed regular feed, and they grew more quickly, too.

Real People, Real Stories

The impact of antibiotics on humankind can be measured in statistics about lives saved. However the drugs' true impact can best be realized in the stories of people who are alive because of them.

Anna Fairly has one such story. In 2009 the German student was working at an internship for the World Health Organization in Copenhagen, Denmark. One day she became very ill and was taken to a hospital, where doctors operated for appendicitis. Instead of getting better, Fairly got much worse as an infection spread throughout her body. Doctors determined the kind of bacteria threatening Fairly was a strain known as *Streptococcus* A. They immediately began treating her with high doses of two antibiotics known to be effective against the bacteria. They also put Fairly in a medically induced coma to prevent brain damage from the infection. It took about forty-eight hours for the antibiotics to begin to take effect, but within two weeks the young woman had completely recovered. "My experience has made me realize how precious antibiotics are," said Fairly after her brush with death. "Greater awareness needs to be made about the importance of using antibiotics effectively. . . . Ultimately we know so little—I never even discovered where the infection I got came from."

Anna Fairly, "Antibiotics Saved My Life," World Health Organization: Regional Office for Europe, 2011. www.euro.who.int.

Jukes was so excited by his discovery that he sent samples of his Aureomycin-laced feed to researchers in agricultural colleges around the country and asked them to try it on their own animals. Science writer Maryn McKenna relates, "They reported back that small doses not only cured a bloody diarrhea that would have killed young pigs, but also tripled their rate of growth and boosted the weight of turkey chicks."[25] As word got out, farmers began begging for the antibiotic feed.

By 1951 the FDA had approved six different antibiotics to be used as growth promoters in animal feed. Then in 1953, the FDA approved the greater use of antibiotics in animal feed to protect the animals from disease. These doses were not large enough to treat an infection, but they prevented animals from getting sick and made it difficult for bacteria to spread among animal populations. As a result, even more chickens survived to make it to slaughterhouses and markets. Chicken was no longer a luxury but a staple in American households. Before antibiotics, people ate chicken on a special occasion, perhaps for Sunday dinner. It became so affordable, however, that people could eat it every day if they wished.

The World's Antibiotic Meat Diet

Antibiotics changed the way America and the world eats. In modern America, people eat more chicken than either beef or pork, but cattle and hogs are raised on antibiotics, too. When cattlemen and hog farmers learned of the tremendous growth and health benefits of antibiotics in chickens, they began using antibiotics on their own animals—either added to their animals' feed or water. With the success of American farmers and ranchers, the practice of adding antibiotics to farm animal feed spread quickly

Most livestock and farmed fish and shrimp (pictured) are given preventive or growth-promoting doses of antibiotics. Experts once believed this practice was perfectly safe.

throughout the Western world. It soon became the standard for raising animals globally; livestock ingest antibiotics from birth until they are sent to the slaughterhouse. As a result, the production of meat everywhere has risen dramatically.

All meat has become more affordable, because most food animals are fed preventive or growth-promoting doses of antibiotics. Even fish and shrimp farming in Asia depends on antibiotics today. All these protein sources are abundant and available, even among many people in the developing world. Globally, more antibiotics are used for dosing animals raised for food than are taken by humans for infections. In the United States, four times as many antibiotics are used in animals as in people.

From the beginning, many researchers, the pharmaceutical industry, and agricultural specialists argued and firmly believed that the farming use of antibiotics was perfectly safe. Indeed it was seen as necessary if the world was to feed its growing population. Nevertheless some scientists worried about what they saw as the overuse and abuse of antibiotics in this way. In 1971 Jukes responded to those critics, "Do we have so many cattle, pigs, and chickens that we ignore the need for feeding them by the most economical means? I do not think so."[26] The FDA seemed to agree—such universal use of antibiotics posed no public health threat that anyone could identify with certainty. The human world embraced their use with little reservation.

CHAPTER 4

The Dark Side

During the golden age of antibiotics, these medicines were thought of as "miracle drugs." But from the beginning, some medical researchers and scientists saw a problem. Antibiotics not only impacted the human world but also had an unintended, unexpected, and enormous impact on the bacterial world. Bacteria adjusted, adapted, and developed resistance to antibiotics—they learned to fight back.

Resistance

In 1945, after winning the Nobel Prize for his discovery of penicillin, Alexander Fleming warned about the dangers of overusing and abusing the antibiotic. He even predicted that bacteria might become resistant to the drug, "It is not difficult to make microbes resistant to penicillin in the laboratory by exposing them to concentrations not sufficient to kill them, and the same thing has occasionally happened in the body," he said. "The time may come when penicillin can be bought by anyone in the shops. Then there is the danger that the ignorant man may easily underdose himself and by exposing his microbes to non-lethal quantities of the drug make them resistant."[27]

Fleming was describing a scenario in which a weak dose of penicillin, or one taken for too few days, kills

45

most pathogenic bacteria—but not all. The susceptible organisms die, but those bacteria that are stronger remain. Those tougher bacteria survive, grow, and multiply as what is called drug-resistant bacteria. This kind of resistance can happen when the sale of antibiotics is unregulated. Without medical advice, people may buy and take the drugs at the wrong dosage or for the wrong length of time, whenever they feel sick. Antibiotics were not classified as prescription drugs in the United States until 1951. In many countries today, it remains legal to purchase antibiotics over the counter, with no prescription. This circumstance may lead to the growth of drug-resistant bacteria that do not respond to antibiotics.

Antibiotic resistance is the ability of bacteria to resist the effects of an antibiotic to which they were previously susceptible. Like all living organisms, bacteria can change their characteristics in response to pressure from their environment. Because of their rapid reproduction rate and their unique ability to easily acquire new traits, they are able to develop antibiotic resistance faster than any medical researchers in Fleming's time could have predicted.

Survival Strategies

As scientists learned more about the bacterial world, they discovered why antibiotic resistance was so difficult to overcome, even with multiple antibiotics available for use. Bacteria are able to share genes for resistance with other bacteria and to acquire genes for resistance from each other. Like people, bacteria have strands of DNA arranged into genes that code for and control their behavior, function, and traits. Bacteria, however, have structures called plasmids, which people and animals do not have. Plasmids are bacteria's secret weapons. Plasmids carry genes for resistance and can be traded with other bacteria. This is called horizontal gene transfer, and it accounts for how resistance is spread among bacteria. So, for example, one staph bacterium can pass its penicillin resistance to a strep bacterium or an *Escherichia coli* bacterium, as well as to other staph bacteria. In addition, a penicillin-resistant staph bacterium can acquire extra plasmids carrying resistance to other antibiotics and become multidrug resistant.

To make matters worse, in the right environment, bacteria can reproduce incredibly rapidly through cell division. *E. coli*, for instance, can reproduce every twenty minutes. This large group of bacteria lives in many environments, including the intestines of animals and people. Most of them are harmless, but some are pathogenic and can cause diarrhea, bloodstream infections, pneumonia, urinary tract infections, and respiratory illnesses. *E. coli* can divide in two, then four, then eight, and so on. Within eight hours, one *E. coli* bacterium can become more than 16 million. That is why bacterial infections can make people sick so fast.

With an effective antibiotic at the correct dosage level, all these bacteria can be wiped out, but not if the bacteria have acquired defense mechanisms for survival. Microbiologist Laura Christine McCaughey explains, "Bacteria and fungi naturally use antibiotics as weapons to kill each other to compete for space

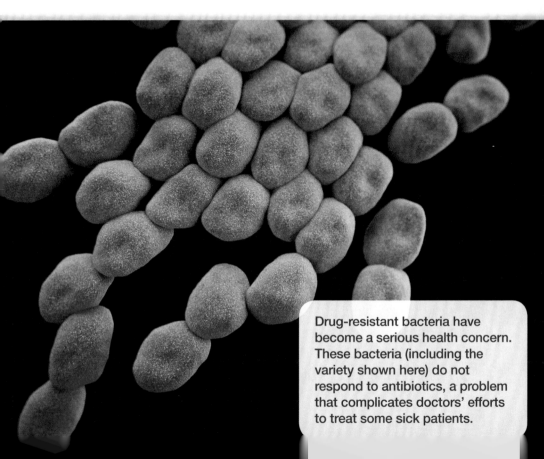

Drug-resistant bacteria have become a serious health concern. These bacteria (including the variety shown here) do not respond to antibiotics, a problem that complicates doctors' efforts to treat some sick patients.

> "Bacteria and fungi naturally use antibiotics as weapons to kill each other to compete for space and food."[28]
>
> —Laura Christine McCaughey, microbiologist

and food; they have been doing this for over a billion years. This means they are used to coming into contact with antibiotics in the environment and developing and sharing antibiotic resistance mechanisms."[28]

One strain of bacteria may carry an uncommon gene that makes it strong and resistant to a drug, and this strain may survive an improper dose of antibiotics when the bacteria without that gene are killed. McCaughey continues, "However, the resistant changes only stay in the bacterial population if the antibiotic is constantly present in the bacteria's environment. Our overuse of antibiotics is resulting in the propagation and maintenance of these changes."[29] This is the kind of antibiotic resistance that Fleming and other scientists feared if antibiotics were overused and abused. Once penicillin was in widespread use, for example, penicillin-resistant strains of bacteria appeared within ten years.

The Battle with Staph Bacteria

The first bacteria to become resistant to penicillin were a type of staph known as *Staphylococcus aureus* (*S. aureus*). *S. aureus* is the most common cause of staph infections in people. Despite this fact, the medical world was not particularly concerned about resistance to penicillin. Physician and medical historian Scott Podolsky of Harvard Medical School explains, "There was an optimism at the time that pharma [drug companies] was going to keep making new drugs. It looked like an arms race, and we could stay one step ahead of the bugs."[30]

For a few years that optimism appeared to be justified. In 1959 the pharmaceutical company Beecham developed methicillin, an antibiotic that worked against penicillin-resistant staph infections. In 1961, however, the first recorded case of methicillin-resistant *S. aureus* appeared in a hospital in the United Kingdom. This case is considered the "birth of MRSA"[31]—which stands for methicillin-resistant *S. aureus*. The first case of MRSA in the United States occurred in 1968. Scientists are unsure how MRSA arose, but they believe it began through horizontal gene transfer.

During the 1970s and 1980s MRSA gradually spread around the world. At first MRSA remained relatively rare and usually infected people in hospitals and nursing homes. Staph infections are common in hospitals because people are already ill and have weakened immune systems that cannot fight infections very well. They also frequently have open wounds, such as from surgery or even needle injections. Staph bacteria normally live on people's skin or in their noses and typically do no harm, but these bacteria

Battling MRSA

Braxe R. was two and a half years old when he developed an ear infection that would not go away. Finally the child's doctor tested a sample of the fluid that was oozing from his ear and discovered MRSA. Braxe was admitted to the hospital, isolated in his room so that the dangerous infection could not spread to other patients, and treated with vancomycin. Vancomycin is an older antibiotic not used commonly today because newer antibiotics are generally more effective and have fewer side effects. However, it can work against MRSA. Braxe received the antibiotic through an intravenous tube (an IV) that dripped the drug into his body through a needle in his arm. After a week in the hospital, he was able to go home with his parents, but every day for the next two weeks, his parents had to hook up the IV for hours at a time to give him continued antibiotic therapy.

The prolonged treatment did not work, and the MRSA infection remained. Braxe's father remembers, "We felt as though we were out of options. Doctors told us they wanted to try a new drug that could help, but noted it could damage Braxe's internal organs because it wasn't made for small children." No one was sure whether the drug would work, but it did—Braxe's case of MRSA had finally been cured. Braxe's experience is not unusual with MRSA infections. Doctors cannot know for sure what antibiotics, if any, will kill the multidrug-resistant bacteria.

Patient Stories, "Braxe R." Infectious Diseases Society of America (IDSA). www.idsociety.org.

can infect hospital patients exposed to them. If the germs are MRSA, instead of normal staph, they become increasingly difficult to treat and can spread from patient to patient. Doctors turned to other antibiotics, such as vancomycin, to treat these hospital outbreaks, but many patients did not survive.

Medical professionals worked diligently to prevent MRSA infections by isolating sick patients and instituting strict rules about sterilizing medical equipment, handwashing, and general hospital sanitation. The Alliance for the Prudent Use of Antibiotics at Tufts University in Boston explains, "Environmentally, antibiotic resistance spreads as bacteria themselves move from place to place; bacteria can travel via airplane, water and wind. People can pass the resistant bacteria to others; for example, by coughing or contact with unwashed hands."[32]

This is probably how MRSA left the hospital setting and moved into the general population during the 1990s. It started as an epidemic of MRSA in Australia, among the Aboriginal people. Europe, the Americas, Asia, and Africa saw the rise of MRSA in their

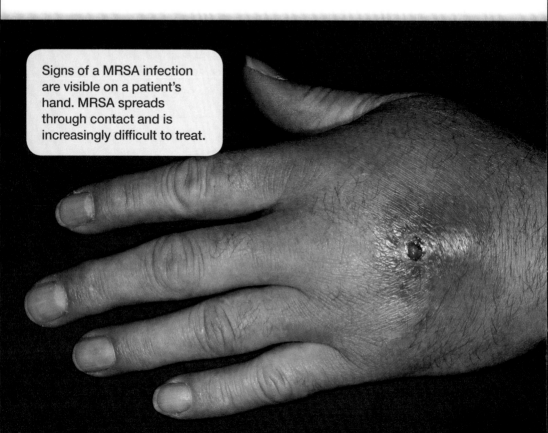

Signs of a MRSA infection are visible on a patient's hand. MRSA spreads through contact and is increasingly difficult to treat.

populations, too, as the outbreaks began to spread around the world. These bacteria came to be called community-associated MRSA, because they arose in the general community among people who had never been hospitalized.

MRSA is now found globally, and continues to pose a threat. It typically affects young, healthy people, leaving them with severe skin infections, bloodstream infections, or pneumonia. People rarely know where they acquired the infection, but researchers have determined that at least two out of every one hundred people today carry MRSA in their noses. Treating MRSA infections is difficult and often requires months of surgeries to remove the infected skin and tissue, as well as multiple antibiotics. Vancomycin is still used, although it can cause serious side effects and allergies in many people. In addition, although it remains rare, a strain of S. aureus resistant to vancomycin was identified in 2002.

> "Environmentally, antibiotic resistance spreads as bacteria themselves move from place to place; bacteria can travel via airplane, water and wind."[32]
>
> —The Alliance for the Prudent Use of Antibiotics

The medical world still has a few antibiotics that successfully treat antibiotic-resistant staph infections; these include drugs such as daptomycin, ceftaroline, and linezolid. These drugs are withheld from common use so that the bacteria will remain unexposed to them and thus stay susceptible, or responsive, to antibiotics. Still, according to the MRSA Research Center of the University of Chicago, ninety thousand Americans are victims of MRSA infections every year, and twenty thousand of them die.

MRSA Is Not the Only Superbug

Staph are not the only bacteria that easily develop antibiotic resistance, and penicillins are not the only class of antibiotics to which the bacterial world has developed resistance. Consider tetracycline, for example, which was made available to the public in 1950. In 1959 a strain of the gram-negative bacteria named

The Genetics of Resistance

In 2017, a research team at the University of Birmingham in the United Kingdom found a gene that helps protect bacteria from antibiotics. The researchers discovered two ways that the gene plays a role in coding for resistance. It protects the bacterium's DNA from being harmed by the class of antibiotics known as fluoroquinolone antibiotics (broad-spectrum antibiotics such as ciprofloxacin and levofloxacin). The gene also stops the antibiotic known as doxycycline from getting inside a bacterium. (Doxycycline is a drug in the tetracycline family.)

Understanding what this bacterial gene does is important because researchers can then experiment with ways of blocking its action. Dr. Prateek Sharma, a member of the research team, explains, "The resistance mechanisms that we identified are found in many different species of bacteria." Someday the researchers hope that knowledge of the gene's actions will help other scientists to develop new antibiotics that can overcome the gene's ability to cause resistance.

University of Birmingham, "New Mechanisms Discovered That Bacteria Use to Protect Themselves from Antibiotics," ScienceDaily, November 13, 2017. www.sciencedaily.com.

Shigella became resistant to tetracycline. Then the bacteria developed resistance to multiple drugs, including ampicillin and ciprofloxacin.

Shigella bacteria cause an intestinal infection called shigellosis, characterized by symptoms of diarrhea, fever, and stomach cramps. It is highly contagious and causes five hundred thousand cases of diarrhea in the United States each year. People usually recover from the disease in about a week, so the CDC now urges doctors not to prescribe any antibiotics for most patients. The idea is that reducing bacterial exposure to antibiotics will eventually decrease resistance. The more often bacteria are exposed to antibiotics, the more likely they are to develop resistance and pass it along to other bacterial populations. It is in this way that antibiotic-resistant bacteria can become common. For those patients who do not get better on their own, the CDC advises doctors to prescribe an antibiotic only after testing a bacterial sample to discover which specific drug will work. So far most shigella bacteria are only partially resistant to doxycycline and streptomycin, so a strong dose of these drugs eventually kills the bacteria.

Rise of the Superbugs

Each kind of pathogenic bacteria has developed resistance to at least one common antibiotic. That means each bacterial disease is untreatable with one or more drugs that used to work. By the beginning of the twenty-first century, antibiotic-resistant bacteria were appearing almost as soon as a new antibiotic was introduced. The injectable antibiotic named daptomycin, for instance, was introduced in 2003 to be used for life-threatening infections of gram-positive bacteria that are resistant to other antibiotics. However, the first evidence of daptomycin-resistant bacteria appeared in 2004. Medical scientists theorize that exposure to antibiotics actually encourages bacteria to share plasmids and spreads resistance more rapidly. Science writer Melinda Wenner Moyer explains, "It is as if the microbes band together in the face of a common enemy, sharing their strongest weapons with their comrades."[33]

"We are fast running out of treatment options."[34]

—Marie-Paule Kieny, WHO assistant director general

The medical world now recognizes that bacteria have not been conquered at all; some even believe that humans are in serious danger of losing the war against infectious disease. Although most diseases are still easily cured with antibiotics, others are increasingly difficult to treat. Bacterial strains have evolved that are resistant to most antibiotics. These bacteria are called superbugs, and in 2017, World Health Organization (WHO) assistant director general Dr. Marie-Paule Kieny warned, "We are fast running out of treatment options."[34]

The Dangers of Overuse

Compounding the problem is that antibiotics continue to be overused. The CDC estimates that 30 percent of antibiotic prescriptions are unnecessary. These prescriptions—47 million a year— are doled out in doctors' offices, clinics, and emergency rooms when they are not needed to cure a bacterial infection. Perhaps the patient demands a medicine and the doctor gives in. Perhaps the doctor worries that the infection might be bacterial in nature and gives the prescription, just to be safe. Many times, however, the sickness is caused by a virus, not bacteria, and antibiotics are useless for viral infections, such as colds and many intestinal illnesses. These sicknesses get better on their own most of the time and do not require antibiotics. In addition, says the CDC, "Antibiotics won't help for some common bacterial infections including most cases of bronchitis, many sinus infections, and some ear infections."[35] Yet antibiotics are prescribed, and thus the problem of resistant bacteria spreads in the human world.

Perhaps the most striking example of how antibiotics can lead to the rise of a superbug is *Clostridium difficile* (*C. diff*). It causes very watery diarrhea and may lead to severe intestinal damage. *C. diff* infections usually set in after a person has been taking antibiotics for a prolonged period for another infection. During this time, all the bacteria in a person's body had been effectively killed, except for the *C. diff* bacteria, which are kept in check by the harmless bacteria in the intestines. *C. diff* bacteria are resistant to the antibiotic and their growth explodes. Stopping antibiotic treatment sometimes works to heal *C. diff*, but often the infection continues. Frequently, treatments with other antibiotics, such as vancomycin, fail to kill the *C. diff* bacteria, and people get sicker and sicker. The CDC rates *C. diff* as an urgent drug-resistant threat that reportedly kills fifteen thousand Americans every year. It is an extremely difficult infection to treat.

Even when an antibiotic seems to work, 30 percent of patients have recurring infections. Currently medical researchers are testing new antibiotics in clinical trials and even searching for a

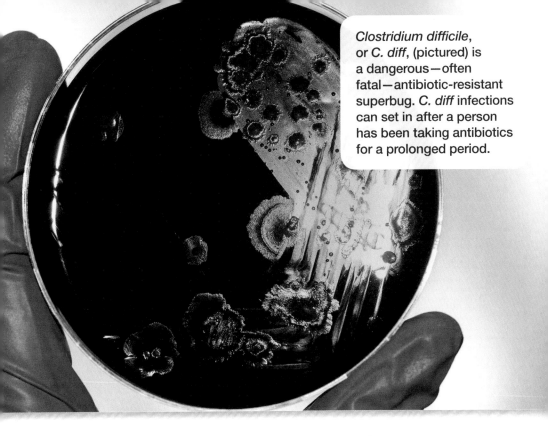

Clostridium difficile, or *C. diff*, (pictured) is a dangerous—often fatal—antibiotic-resistant superbug. *C. diff* infections can set in after a person has been taking antibiotics for a prolonged period.

possible *C. diff* vaccine. When all else fails, some doctors are performing fecal microbial transplantation. This treatment involves acquiring clean feces (poop) from a healthy person with healthy bacteria and transplanting the material into the patient's colon. In some patients this is the only method that seems to stop the infection. One woman named Dina, for example, had a fecal transplant in 2014, after nine years of suffering from *C. diff* and multiple rounds of antibiotics. At age fifty-one, she finally could say, "My life is beginning again because I had the opportunity to have a Fecal Microbial Transplant."[36] The medical world is not certain that fecal microbial transplantation will permanently cure *C. diff*, but prevention of the infection by curbing the overuse of antibiotics is now a priority for many *C. diff* specialists.

From the Farm to People?

At one time scientists believed that antibiotic overuse in people was the primary cause of antibiotic resistance in bacteria. Now, however, they recognize that overuse in agriculture is a major problem, too. When animals are fed antibiotics from birth, they can develop antibiotic-resistant bacteria in their intestines. Then these bacteria are deposited into the soil or on the barn floor in their manure or droppings. Farmers may use the manure to fertilize their fields. Contaminating bacteria may end up on the animals' bodies or on the farmer's shoes or picked up by flies that carry them to new places. Maryn McKenna explains, "Resistant bacteria move from animals to humans in groundwater and dust, on flies, and via the meat those animals get turned into."[37]

In 2011, for instance, the FDA analyzed the bacteria on meats, such as chicken breasts and hamburger. It found tetracycline-resistant bacteria on at least half of them. It also found pork chops carrying bacteria that were resistant to five different antibiotics. People can be infected by these resistant bacteria if they ingest meat that is undercooked (so that the bacteria survive) or fail to adequately wash their hands after handling the meat.

Researchers cannot yet prove that farming is responsible for the rise of resistant bacterial infections in people. However, they theorize that the crowded conditions in which livestock are raised enable resistant genes to pass into the soil and from one animal to another very rapidly. And since animal manure is used to fertilize fields to grow crops, they believe that resistant bacteria from the animals are carried to that soil, too. Many people fear that overuse of antibiotics in animals is encouraging the rise of super-bugs that will eventually cause untreatable human diseases.

CHAPTER 5

The Future of Antibiotics

In August 2016, a seventy-year-old woman was admitted to a Nevada hospital with symptoms of a serious infection. Prior to her admission, the woman had been traveling in India for two years, where she had broken her leg and hip. She had surgery in a hospital in India, and soon thereafter her hip became swollen and inflamed. Once she returned to the United States, the infection began to spread throughout her bloodstream. Doctors started antibiotic treatment immediately, but the woman did not respond.

Laboratory analysis of the bacteria in her blood indicated that the infection was caused by a type of Enterobacteriaceae, a class of bacteria that includes such pathogens as *E. coli*, *Salmonella*, and *Shigella*. Making matters worse, her type of Enterobacteriaceae appeared to be resistant to carbapenem, a modern, powerful, broad-spectrum antibiotic that is mostly used to treat antibiotic-resistant bacteria.

Carbapenem-resistant Enterobacteriaceae (CRE) is an extremely serious infection, because it does not respond to most antibiotics—and it can be fatal if left untreated. CRE kills up to 50 percent of patients when it gets into the bloodstream. "CRE are nightmare bacteria," said then CDC director Tom Frieden. "Our strongest antibiotics don't work and patients are left with potentially untreatable infections."[38] The type of CRE that this woman contracted was even worse. It was not only multi-drug resistant, but pandrug resistant. Pandrug-resistant bacteria do not respond to any known antibiotics. Such bacteria are unusual, and the woman was the first US patient to be hospitalized with this kind of infection. Her doctors had no treatment options for their patient at all, and she died in the hospital after about two months. Doctors and scientists fear that such outcomes will become increasingly common unless drug resistance in bacteria can be overcome.

A Post-Antibiotic Era?

Although still rare, cases of CRE are terrifying to medical researchers and physicians, because they represent the possibility of a post-antibiotic future—a time when bacteria have won the war against humans' best defenses against them. "We talk about a pre-antibiotic era and an antibiotic era," said Frieden in 2013. "If we're not careful, we will soon be in a post-antibiotic era. And, in fact, for some patients and some microbes, we are already there."[39]

> "We talk about a pre-antibiotic era and an antibiotic era. If we're not careful, we will soon be in a post-antibiotic era."[39]
>
> —Tom Frieden, CDC director

Throughout the medical world, the fear of a post-antibiotic era is very real. What if all bacteria become pandrug resistant? What if all bacteria become like CRE? Already hospitals are careful to isolate patients who have multidrug-resistant infections, lest the infections spread to other people and throughout the community. Doctors reserve their most powerful antibiotics to treat these very resistant infections. But if the day comes when *no* antibiotics work against even the most common infections, doctors worry that the future will start to look like the past. "Antibiotic resistance puts all of the progress we have made—in improving public health and quality of life, in combating infectious disease, and in modernizing health

Bacteria Eaters

Bacteriophages are viruses that attack and kill bacteria, and in the future they may be a potent weapon in the fight against drug-resistant bacteria. Bacteriophages slip inside bacterial cells. Then, like all viruses, they hijack the bacterium's DNA and replace it with their own. In this way, the bacteriophages are able to make more of themselves until there are so many that the bacterial wall bursts and releases the viruses to infect more bacteria.

Bacteriophages cannot infect any cells other than bacteria. In fact each type of bacteriophage can only infect a specific kind or strain of bacteria. Each bacterium—whether staph or strep or *E. coli*—has its own bacteria eater to which it is vulnerable. (Bacteriophage means "bacteria eater.") Some scientists believe that bacteriophage mixtures could be developed from viruses that kill the bacteria most likely to infect people. The bacteriophages would destroy even multidrug-resistant bacteria, thus solving the problem of antibiotic resistance. Bacteriophage therapy has been used in Russia and a few eastern European countries for years. Today some scientists in the Western world are researching the value of bacteriophages instead of or along with antibiotics. Others doubt the usefulness of these viruses. They argue that there is only weak scientific evidence of their effectiveness and safety in humans and that it would be too difficult to make a mixture with the exact bacteriophages required for each specific infection.

care—at risk," says Anne Schuchat of the CDC. "The threat of antibiotic resistance is like a time machine that takes us back to when simple infections were deadly."[40]

Consequences of Pandrug Resistance

In a post-antibiotic era, life would be quite different than it is today—and not just because there would be no treatment for bacterial infections. Many other medicines and procedures would become either highly dangerous or impossible. For example, all surgeries that involve opening the body to the outside environment carry a risk of infection. No matter how careful a surgeon is, there is a chance that a stray bacterium will enter the wound, either during

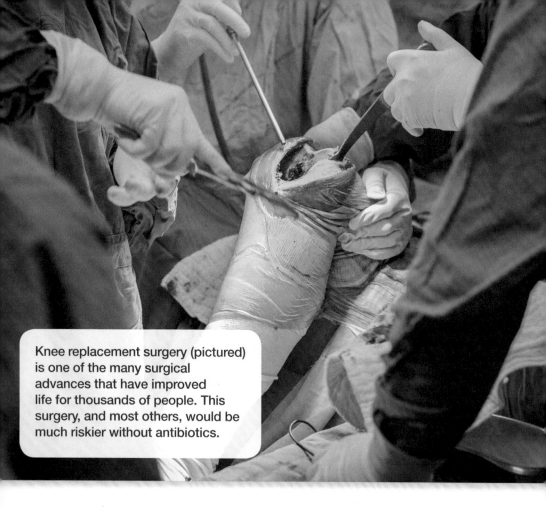

Knee replacement surgery (pictured) is one of the many surgical advances that have improved life for thousands of people. This surgery, and most others, would be much riskier without antibiotics.

or after surgery. For that reason, anyone who has surgery is given a course of antibiotics before and after the operation. This practice prevents any bacterial invasion. In a post-antibiotic era, however, surgery probably would have to be avoided at all costs, except in life or death situations. The threat of infection would simply be too dangerous.

Without antibiotics, many invasive life-saving and live-improving medical procedures might be impossible. To help critically ill patients breathe, for example, a tube attached to a ventilator is inserted through the nose or mouth and into the trachea (windpipe). And joint replacements, although fairly routine, require incisions. Devices such as catheters and ports (thin tubes that are threaded through blood vessels and appliances connected to tubes) are implanted under the skin so that patients who need frequent drug injections or blood tests do not have to be repeatedly stuck with needles. These and other invasive procedures always carry a small risk of infection, but if infections were untreatable, few doctors—or patients—would take the risk. Life-saving procedures such as heart valve replacements would become too risky to perform. One British research group estimates that one out of every six patients undergoing hip joint replacement would die in a post-antibiotic future.

Treatments for cancer and other chronic illnesses would radically change, too. Chemotherapy and radiation therapy, along with many other drugs, suppress the body's immune system. This means that the person cannot fight off infecting microorganisms that typically pose no threat to a healthy immune system. Organ transplants, including kidney, bone marrow, and liver transplantation, also require suppressing the immune system—often throughout the person's lifetime. Patients must take immunosuppressant drugs so that their immune systems will not attack the transplanted organ as if it were a foreign invader. Antibiotics are necessary to protect immunosuppressed patients from infection. In a post-antibiotic era, however, having a suppressed immune system would be as deadly as whatever condition the doctors were trying to treat. Dr. Michael Bell of the CDC says, "We deal with that risk now by loading people up with broad-spectrum antibiotics, sometimes for weeks at a stretch. But if you can't do that, the decision to treat somebody takes on a different ethical tone."[41]

Even very simple, nonmedical procedures would become extraordinarily dangerous should antibiotics not be available to treat the rare infections that might occur. People would likely think twice about piercing their ears or getting a tattoo. Cosmetic outpatient procedures might end completely. "Right now, if you want to be a sharp-looking hipster and get a tattoo, you're not putting your life on the line," says Bell. "Botox injections, liposuction, those become possibly life-threatening. Even driving to work: We rely on antibiotics to make a major accident something we can get through, as opposed to a death sentence."[42]

How to Prevent a Post-Antibiotic Future

Experts estimate that if nothing is done, by 2050 about 10 million people will be dying each year from antibiotic-resistant infections. A post-antibiotic future sounds grim—but it is not too late; the loss of effective antibiotics is not inevitable. Many international organizations, government leaders, medical researchers, and pharmaceutical companies are working to make sure that the treasure of antibiotics is not lost for future generations. One important approach is to begin to reduce overuse of antibiotics worldwide. It will be impossible to prevent the advent of drug-resistant bacteria entirely. As microbiology expert Jason Tetro explains, "Antibiotic resistance cannot be stopped because it is a natural part of bacterial life."[43] However, multidrug and pandrug resistance are not normal. People can stop exposing bacteria to so many antibiotics, and thus make resistance more rare.

In the United Kingdom, under the leadership of England's chief medical officer, Sally Davies, health officials are urged to prescribe antibiotics only when necessary. In addition, the United Kingdom is leading a drive for global awareness of the problem of antibiotic resistance. In one year, for example, between 2014 and 2015, the United Kingdom reported a reduction in antibiotic use of 4.3 percent. That may not seem like much, but it constitutes progress in terms of persuading people to stop taking antibiotics for nonbacterial illnesses and doctors to stop prescribing them without evidence that they are necessary. "We estimate that about one in three or one in four prescriptions in primary care are probably not needed," says Davies. "But other countries use vastly more antibiotics in the community and they need to start doing as we are, which is reducing usage."[44] That is why Davies is urging health officials worldwide to raise awareness about the dangers of overusing antibiotics. She is also helping to lead an international project to track and map the spread of superbugs globally, to discover where the problem is most acute, and to learn how widespread the superbugs are.

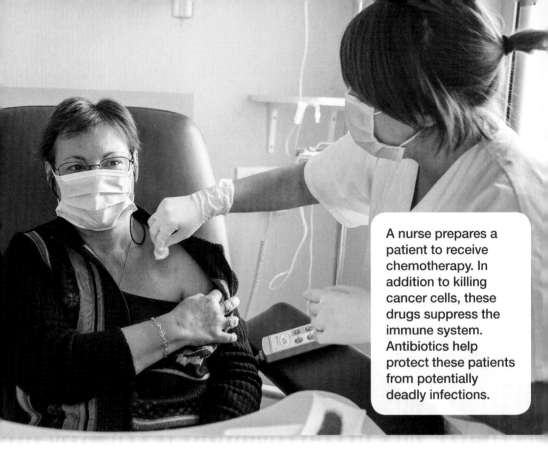

A nurse prepares a patient to receive chemotherapy. In addition to killing cancer cells, these drugs suppress the immune system. Antibiotics help protect these patients from potentially deadly infections.

In the United States, the CDC supports a nationwide drive to reduce antibiotic prescriptions. Part of the program involves reaching out to physicians and improving public health education. As of 2018, however, the CDC had been unable to report a decline in antibiotic use. The agency has been instrumental in establishing the National Action Plan for Combating Antibiotic-Resistant Bacteria, a government effort to understand the problem of antibiotic resistance. It is also developing rapid diagnostic tests for the presence of specific bacteria so that infections can be appropriately treated and is working to prevent the spread of pandrug-resistant bacteria in the population.

Protection Inside the Body

The CDC and other medical agencies continue to urge the public to stop demanding antibiotic prescriptions when they are ill. Taking antibiotics when unnecessary has a detrimental effect on the individual patient as well as the public health. Each person has billions of both harmless and beneficial bacteria living on and in his or her body. Bacteria are especially numerous in the intestines. Together these microorganisms make up what is called the human microbiota, and the beneficial ones are essential for each person's life and health. They help the body digest food and manufacture some necessary vitamins. The community of beneficial microbes also helps keep harmful bacteria from establishing a community and growing out of control.

When a person takes antibiotics, many of these beneficial bacteria are killed. The overuse of antibiotics actually destroys the protection the microbiota provides, making it easier for pathogenic bacteria to multiply and cause sickness, and for even a few resistant ones to spread through the body and cause infection. Scientists are still learning how the microbiota functions and the role it plays in human health. But they are beginning to understand that a healthy microbiota could be an essential weapon in the fight against a post-antibiotic future. The Baylor College of Medicine states, "It may be possible to treat a bacterial infection caused by a 'bad' bacterial species by promoting the growth of the 'good' bacteria."[45]

New, Better Antibiotics

Good bacteria may someday be used to stop infections by bad bacteria, but other researchers are striving to discover more new antibiotics. While new antibiotics cannot stop resistance, they can keep humans one step ahead in the continual war against bacteria. Researchers are still reviewing soil samples in the hopes of finding new kinds of bacterial chemicals that can fight pathogenic bacteria. Microbiologist Sean Brady is undertaking such work. He studies bacterial genes using the same genome sequencing techniques that allow scientists to identify genes in people. Instead of growing cultures of bacteria, Brady and his research team analyze the DNA that they find in soil samples. Their goal is to find powerful antibiotic chemicals.

A Surprising Idea

In 2017 ten highly respected British disease specialists, led by Professor Martin Llewelyn of the Brighton and Sussex Medical School, issued some advice that startled the medical community: the decades-old advice to finish a full course of prescribed antibiotics is wrong. They suggested that patients should only take antibiotics until they feel better and then stop.

Most medical doctors were shocked by this advice. Since antibiotics were discovered, the fear has been that taking too little of them kills weak bacteria and allows the stronger ones to survive. The British experts, however, say this belief is not supported by strong evidence. Instead they argue that long, complete courses of antibiotics are unnecessary, and that they represent antibiotics overuse and encourage pathogenic bacteria to multiply. Furthermore, complete courses of antibiotics kill the beneficial and harmless bacteria on the skin and in the intestines, leaving space for dangerous bacteria to grow. The longer people take antibiotics, they suggested, the more likely it is that antibiotic resistance is fueled. More research on this idea is needed, but many experts believe it is time to reconsider the way antibiotics are prescribed and the duration of their use.

In 2018 the team announced that they found genes that code for molecules of a substance called malacidin. "They are brand new molecules," said Brady. "They have never been seen before."[46] Malacidins are a whole new class of antibiotics that attack bacteria in a different way. Instead of penetrating the cell wall, they interfere with the cell's ability to reform its protective wall after cell division. Brady and his team tested the malacidin compound they developed on lab animals. The drug successfully killed bacterial infections in the animals, including MRSA. So far, bacteria exposed to malacidin seem to be unable to develop resistance against the compound.

Malacidins are very promising substances that may someday lead to a new, powerful antibiotic for people. Scientists are hopeful about the findings, and Brady is continuing his research, trying to improve the effectiveness of the compound. However, this work is painstaking. "It is impossible to say when, or even if, an early stage antibiotic discovery like the malacidins will proceed to the clinic," he says. "It is a long, arduous road from the initial discovery of an antibiotic to a clinically used entity."[47] If malacidins do prove safe and effective, however, the world will have a new drug that works against drug-resistant gram-positive bacteria. New antibiotics for drug-resistant gram-negative bacteria are still needed, and other researchers are searching the world's soils for other promising substances.

Pharmaceutical companies are also now searching for and developing new antibiotics. In 2016 about one hundred companies signed an international commitment called the Davos Declaration, promising to "reduce the development of antimicrobial resistance, invest in research and development of new treatments and diagnostics, and improve access to current and new antibiotics."[48] As of 2018 several new antibiotics were in clinical trials for such bacterial diseases as multidrug-resistant tuberculosis, gram-negative urinary tract infections, pneumonia, and CRE. Governments are helping these efforts by shortening the time and application requirements for new antibiotics. This fast track approval strategy is used by the FDA to prioritize certain badly needed drugs, review them quickly, and speed the agency's approval of them. Fast tracking helps drug companies reduce the cost of getting a new drug on the market.

Reforming Agricultural Practices

New antibiotics could help people who have drug-resistant bacterial infections, but they do not address the rise of resistant bacteria from antibiotics used in agriculture. No one objects to giving antibiotics to animals that are sick with infections. But giving them to animals as preventative medicine, or to make them bigger or stronger, is still widespread practice. However, the use of antibiotics in these ways is beginning to change. In 2006 the European Union banned the use of antibiotics to promote growth in livestock. In 2008 Denmark banned the use of antibiotics in all healthy animals, and the Netherlands followed in 2009. In 2017 the US FDA banned the use of growth-promoting antibiotics in animals, though using antibiotics to preempt illness remains legal. That means antibiotics can still be vastly overused in some places.

Agricultural use of antibiotics remains an issue, and yet some food companies are responding voluntarily to the urgings of scientists and the public. As public awareness of the antibiotic crisis has grown, agricultural practices have changed, even without government regulation. In 2016, for example, Perdue Farms, a major chicken producer, announced that it was ending the routine use of antibiotics on all its farms. The company has stopped using antibiotics except when any chickens are actually sick, which

Some food producers are heeding the warnings of health experts who say that use of antibiotics to promote growth is contributing to a global health crisis. At least two major US chicken producers have announced they are ending the routine use of these drugs.

"Our consumers have already told us they want chicken raised without any antibiotics."[49]

—Jim Perdue, chairman of Perdue Farms

happens only about 5 percent of the time. Jim Perdue, the chairman of the company, said, "Our consumers have already told us they want chicken raised without any antibiotics." Now almost all Perdue chicken can be sold with the label "no antibiotics ever," or "NAE."[49] Tyson Foods followed suit in 2017, announcing no antibiotics used in all its chicken products. Several other companies are doing the same, and despite the fears of some, the animals remain healthy, while the cost of raising them has not become prohibitively expensive.

Saving Antibiotics

Worldwide the problem of antibiotic resistance has not gone away, but progress is being made to avoid a post-antibiotic future. Everyone can help keep antibiotics effective by buying NAE foods, taking antibiotics only when necessary, and protecting their own microbiota and keeping it healthy. Progress may be slow, but many scientists believe that antibiotics can be used responsibly—and their wonderful benefits can be preserved for future generations.

Introduction: Saved by the Millions

1. Laura Helmuth, "Why Are You Not Dead Yet?," *Slate*, September 5, 2013. www.slate.com.
2. Maryn McKenna, "Imagining the Post-antibiotics Future," Medium, FERNnews, November 20, 2013. https://medium.com/@fernnews.

Chapter 1: War with Germs

3. Quoted in University of California Museum of Paleontology, "Antony van Leeuwenhoek (1632–1723)." www.ucmp.berkeley.edu.
4. Quoted in Robert P. Gaynes, *Germ Theory: Medical Pioneers in Infectious Diseases*. Washington, DC: ASM, 2011. Kindle Edition.
5. Quoted in iWonder, "Louis Pasteur: The Man Who Led the Fight Against Germs," BBC. www.bbc.co.uk.
6. Quoted in Paul de Kruif, *Microbe Hunters.* New York: Harcourt Brace, 1926, p. 94.
7. Quoted in Robert P. Gaynes, *Germ Theory: Medical Pioneers in Infectious Diseases*.
8. Quoted in Robert P. Gaynes, *Germ Theory: Medical Pioneers in Infectious Diseases*.
9. Eric Oatman, "The Drug that Changed the World," *P&S,* Winter, 2005. www.cumc.columbia.edu/ps journal.

Chapter 2: The Golden Age of Antibiotics

10. Quoted in Enrique Raviña, *The Evolution of Drug Discovery: From Traditional Medicines to Modern Drugs*. Weinheim, Germany: Wiley-VCH, 2011, p. 276.
11. Quoted in Nicole Kresge, Robert D. Simoni, and Robert L. Hill, "Selman Waksman: The Father of

Antibiotics," *Journal of Biological Chemistry*, November 26, 2004, vol. 279, no. 48, p. 102. www.jbc.org.

12. George Wong, "The Aftermath of Penicillin," Botany 135, University of Hawaii, 2003. www.botany.hawaii.edu.

13. Quoted in Andrew Meacham, "Lloyd Conover, Who Invented Tetracycline and Was My Stepfather, Dies at 93," *Tampa Bay (FL) Times*, March 15, 2017. www.tampabay.com.

14. Quoted in Andrew Meacham, "Lloyd Conover, Who Invented Tetracycline and Was My Stepfather, Dies at 93."

15. Robert P. Gaynes, *Germ Theory: Medical Pioneers in Infectious Diseases*.

Chapter 3: The Impact of Antibiotics

16. Quoted in Scott H. Podolsky, *The Antibiotic Era: Reform, Resistance, and the Pursuit of a Rational Therapeutics.* Baltimore: Johns Hopkins University Press, 2015, p. 51.

17. Quoted in Scott H. Podolsky, *The Antibiotic Era: Reform, Resistance, and the Pursuit of a Rational Therapeutics*, p. 56.

18. Quoted in Scott H. Podolsky, *The Antibiotic Era: Reform, Resistance, and the Pursuit of a Rational Therapeutics*, p. 69.

19. Quoted in Suzanne White Junod, PhD, "FDA and Clinical Drug Trials: A Short History," US Food & Drug Administration, February 1, 2018. www.fda.gov.

20. Michelle Meadows, "Promoting Safe & Effective Drugs for 100 Years," *FDA Consumer Magazine*, January–February, 2006. www.fda.gov.

21. Robin Walsh, "A History of the Pharmaceutical Industry," Pharmaphorum, October 1, 2010. https://pharmaphorum.com.

22. Arthur H. Daemmrich and Mary Ellen Bowden, "The Pharmaceutical Golden Era: 1930–60," *Chemical & Engineering News*, vol. 83, no. 25, June 20, 2005. https://cen.acs.org.

23. George Wong, "The Aftermath of Penicillin."

24. Quoted in Robin Walsh, "A History of the Pharmaceutical Industry."

25. Maryn McKenna, "The Chicken Experiment That Shook the World," book excerpt published in undark.org, October 6, 2017. https://undark.org.

26. Maryn McKenna, "The Chicken Experiment That Shook the World."

Chapter 4: The Dark Side

27. Quoted in Uppsala University, "Antibiotic Resistance," Antibiotic Resistance: The Silent Tsunami: Online Course. www.futurelearn.com.
28. Laura Christine McCaughey, "We Know *Why* Bacteria Become Resistant to Antibiotics, but *How* Does This Actually Happen?," The Conversation, June 10, 2016. http://theconversation.com.
29. Laura Christine McCaughey, "We Know *Why* Bacteria Become Resistant to Antibiotics, but *How* Does This Actually Happen?"
30. Quoted in Carl Zimmer, "The Surprising History of the War on Superbugs—and What It Means for the World Today," STAT, September 12, 2016. www.statnews.com.
31. National Institute of Allergy and Infectious Diseases (NIAID) "History, Methicillin-Resistant *Staphylococcus Aureus*, Antimicrobial Resistance," March 8, 2016. www.niaid.nih.gov.
32. Alliance for the Prudent Use of Antibiotics, "General Background: About Antibiotic Resistance," 2014. http://emerald.tufts.edu.
33. Melinda Wenner Moyer, "How Drug-Resistant Bacteria Travel from the Farm to Your Table," *Scientific American*, December 1, 2016. www.scientificamerican.com.
34. Quoted in Donald G. McNeil, Jr. "Deadly, Drug-Resistant 'Superbugs' Pose Huge Threat, W.H.O. Says," *New York Times*, February 27, 2017. www.nytimes.com.
35. Centers for Disease Control and Prevention, "Be Antibiotics Aware: Smart Use, Best Care," December 15, 2017. www.cdc.gov.
36. Quoted in OpenBiome, "My Experience with C. diff and FMT—Dina's Story," May 14, 2014. www.openbiome.org.
37. Maryn McKenna, "Imagining the Post-antibiotics Future."

Chapter 5: The Future of Antibiotics

38. Quoted in Press Release, "CDC: Action Needed Now to Halt Spread of Deadly Bacteria," Centers for Disease Control and Prevention, March 5, 2013. www.cdc.gov.

39. Quoted in Press Briefing Transcript, "CDC Telebriefing on To-day's Drug-Resistant Health Threats," Centers for Disease Control and Prevention, September 16, 2013. www.cdc.gov.

40. Quoted in The Pew Charitable Trusts: Interview, "How CDC Is Combating Antibiotic-Resistant Bacteria," April 3, 2018. www.pewtrusts.org.

41. Quoted in Maryn McKenna, "Imagining the Post-antibiotics Future."

42. Quoted in Maryn McKenna, "Imagining the Post-antibiotics Future."

43. Jason Tetro, "5 Ways You Can Help Prevent the Post-antibiotic Era," *The Blog, Huffington Post Canada*, October 3, 2016. www.huffingtonpost.ca.

44. Quoted in Ella Pickover, "World Leaders Urged to Act on 'Post-antibiotic Apocalypse' by Chief Medical Officer," *Independent* (London), October 12, 2017. www.independent.co.uk.

45. Molecular Virology and Microbiology Faculty, "The Human Microbiome Project," Baylor College of Medicine. www.bcm.edu.

46. Quoted in Rockefeller University News, "Molecule Discovered in Dirt Could Help Against Multi-resistant Bacteria, March 8, 2018. www.rockefeller.edu.

47. Quoted in BBC News, "New Antibiotic Family Discovered in Dirt," February 13, 2018. www.bbc.com.

48. Quoted in Jop de Vrieze, "This New Index Ranks Compa-nies' Efforts in the Fight Against Antimicrobial Resistance," *Science*, January 23, 2018. www.sciencemag.org.

49. Quoted in Dan Charles, "Perdue Goes (Almost) Antibiotic-Free," NPR, October 7, 2016. www.npr.org.

actinomycetes: A large group of gram-positive bacteria from which numerous antibiotics have been created.

broad-spectrum antibiotic: An antibiotic that acts against a wide range of pathogenic bacteria.

gram-negative bacteria: Bacteria that do not retain the dye used to stain them because of their thin cell walls.

gram-positive bacteria: Bacteria that retain the violet dye used to stain them because of their thick cell walls.

horizontal gene transfer: The movement of genetic material not through reproduction but through contact between organisms, either of the same or different species.

immune system: The complex network of cells, tissues, and organs that the body uses to protect itself from invading foreign substances, such as pathogenic bacteria and viruses.

microbiology: The branch of biology that deals with microorganisms.

molecules: The smallest unit of a chemical compound or element. Molecules are composed of atoms bonded together.

pathogen: A microorganism that can cause disease.

plasmid: A small circular strand of DNA in the cytoplasm of a bacterium. Plasmids replicate independently of the bacterium's central DNA.

Books

Jonathan Adams, *Antibiotics*. New York: Cavendish Square, 2017.

Jeanette Farrell, *Invisible Enemies: Stories of Infectious Disease*. New York: Square Fish, 2016.

Connie Goldsmith, *Pandemic: How Climate, the Environment, and Superbugs Increase the Risk*. Minneapolis: Twenty-First Century Books, 2018.

Rebecca E. Hirsch, *The Human Microbiome: The Germs That Keep You Healthy*. Minneapolis: Twenty-First Century Books, 2016.

Katharina Smundak, *The Truth Behind Antibiotics, Pesticides, and Hormones* (From Factory to Table: What You're Really Eating). New York: Rosen, 2018.

Tamara Thompson, ed., *Superbugs*. Farmington Hills, MI: Greenhaven Press, 2016.

Internet Sources

American Chemical Society National Historic Chemical Landmarks, "Selman Waksman and Antibiotics," 2005. www.acs.org/content/acs/en/education/whatischemistry/landmarks/selmanwaksman.html.

Carole Bos, "Alexander Fleming and Penicillin—'the Wonder Drug,'" AwesomeStories.com, May 25, 2015. www.awesomestories.com/asset/view/Alexander-Fleming-and-Penicillin-The-Wonder-Drug-.

Centers for Disease Control and Prevention, "Antibiotic Resistance Questions and Answers," December 7, 2017. www.cdc.gov/antibiotic-use/community/about/antibiotic-resistance-faqs.html.

Khan Academy, "What Is Antibiotic Resistance?," www.khanac ademy.org/science/health-and-medicine/current-issues-in-health -and-medicine/antibiotics-and-antibiotic-resistance/a/what-is -antibiotic-resistance.

Kids' Health, "What About Antibiotics?," Women's and Children's Health Network, www.cyh.com/HealthTopics/HealthTopicDetails Kids.aspx?p=335&np=285&id=2376.

Jason Tetro, "5 Ways You Can Help Prevent The Post-antibiotic Era," *The Blog, Huffington Post Canada*, October 3, 2016. www .huffingtonpost.ca/jason-tetro/5-post-antibiotic-era-tips_b_1226 3742.html.

Websites

Alliance for the Prudent Use of Antibiotics (https://apua.org). This organization is dedicated to containing antibiotic resistance and educating everyone about appropriate antibiotic use. Follow the menu links at the top of the page to learn about resistance and how it develops, the latest research into antibiotic resistance, and personal hygiene issues.

Bacteria World (www.bacteria-world.com). At this site, visitors can learn about all different kinds of bacteria, from beneficial to harmless to pathogenic. Many photos are available that illustrate the variety of bacterial shapes and structures.

Gut Microbiota for Health (www.gutmicrobiotaforhealth.com). From the European Society for Neurogastroenterology & Motility, this site describes the microbial populations living inside human intestines and how and why they are important for health.

Microbiology Online (http://microbiologyonline.org). Learn about microbes of all sorts at this website from the Microbiology Society of Europe. There are sections for teachers and students, with information, videos, and photos about the microscopic world.

World Health Organization (www.who.int). Explore this site for global information about any topic related to health and disease, including infection control, antibiotic resistance, and the top ten causes of mortality worldwide.

INDEX

Note: Boldface page numbers indicate illustrations.

actinomycetes, 22–24
agriculture
 antibiotics in, 41–44
  drug resistance and
   overuse of, 55–56
  reforming practices in,
   66–68, **67**
Alexander, Albert, 19
Alliance for the Prudent
 Use of Antibiotics (Tufts
 University), 50, 75
American Chemical
 Society, 38–39
anthrax, 11
antibiotic resistance,
 45–46
 course of prescription
  and, 65
 genetics of, 52
 multidrug, 46–47, **47,**
  49, 66
 overuse of antibiotics
  and, 54–55
 pandrug, 58, 63
 in Shigella, 51–53
 in staphylococcus,
  48–51

antibiotic(s)
 in agriculture, 41–44
  drug resistance and
   overuse of, 55–56
  reforming practices in,
   66–68, **67**
 broad spectrum, 34–35
 CDC on prescribing,
  52–53
 definition of, 17
 important events in
  history of, **4–5**
 life without, 7–9, 59–61
 modification of, 29
 new developments in,
  40–41
 overuse of, 36–37, 44,
  48, 54
 patented, marketing of,
  34
 synthetic, 30
Aureomycin, 29, 31,
 41–42

bacitracin, 27
bacteria
 development of drug
  resistance in, 46–48,
  52
 diversity of, 21–22
 drug-resistant strains of

PICTURE CREDITS

Cover: 6okean/iStock.com

4: Aninna/Shutterstock.com (top)

4: Jevtic/iStock.com (bottom)

5: Nipaporn Panyacharoen/Shutterstock.com (top)

5: nobeastsofierce/Shutterstock.com (bottom left)

5: SuzanneWrightKY/iStock.com (bottom right)

8: jackscoldsweat/iStock.com

12: Louis Pasteur (1822–95) in his Laboratory, 1885 (oil on canvas), Edelfelt, Albert Gustaf Aristides (1854–1905) / Musee d'Orsay, Paris, France/ Bridgeman Images

16: Associated Press

19: Penicillin was first mass produced in America (color litho), English School, (20th century)/Private Collection/© Look and Learn/Bridgeman Images

23: National Cancer Institute/Science Source

26: Scott Camazine/Science Source

28: Dennis Kunkel Microscopy/Science Source

37: Otis Historical Archives, National Museum of Health and Medicine/Science Source

40: John Hadfield/Science Source

43: Phensri Ngamsommitr/Shutterstock.com

47: CDC/Science Source

50: Scott Camazine/Science Source

55: Louise Murray/Science Source

60: Samrith Na Lumpoon/Shutterstock.com

63: Véronique Burger/Science Source

67: David Tadevosian/Shutterstock.com